That We May Be One

God's plan for the Church to be one in Him

Rod Butterworth

To My Wonderful Wife Linda,
Our Children, Grandchildren,
And All Who Have a Passion
For God's People to Become One.

*"I do not pray for these alone, but also for those who will believe in Me through their word; **that they all may be one**, as You, Father, are in Me, and I in You; that they also may be one in Us, that the world may believe that You sent Me"*
(Jesus Christ, John 17:20,21).

"We should never bend the Scriptures to fit our theology.
We should bend our theology to fit the Scriptures."
Rod Butterworth

CONTENTS

Introduction

Jesus is praying for all the Christians of America. Of course He is! The Bible indicates He is interceding for true believers everywhere at all times. The focus of this book is to encourage spiritual renewal and restoration of God's people in this amazing but critical time of precariousness for the United States of America—and for Christians worldwide. Jesus must have a huge prayer list!

Do I believe that this writing will produce any dramatic effects to bring together in unity the different streams of Christianity that have developed divisiveness over the last several hundred years? Many have been the attempts. Well, all things are possible with God, but only when the right kind of prayer, humility, and faith are applied.

What is the right kind of faith? It can only be the kind that Jesus is pleased with as seen in the Gospel accounts. The biblical principles presented in this writing on the extremely important subject of corporate unity will be applicable to Christians everywhere. For those who seriously ponder the state of twenty-first-century American culture with spiritual discernment, it is clear to see that the enemy of God is exerting all his power and influence to destroy not only the Church in every way possible, but even the entire country of America. Young people in schools, colleges and universities are literally being taught to hate America and the Judeo-Christian biblical principles upon which she was founded.

Question: Can the enemy of God and his evil work ever be pushed back into ineffectiveness in communities across our country? Absolutely! You can read evidence of such victories over the powers of darkness in both the Old and New Testaments. Small minorities have gained great victories over large majorities—remember Gideon and his three hundred. The key is being on the right side. Let us take hold with active faith the words of truth God has given His people through the words of Jesus Christ:

"Behold, I give you the authority to trample on serpents and scorpions, and over all the power of the enemy, and nothing shall by any means hurt you" (Luke 10:19).

From the Apostle Paul:
"Above all, taking the shield of faith with which you will be able to quench all the fiery darts of the wicked one" (Ephesians 6:16).

From the Psalmist:
"I will fear no evil; for You are with me; Your rod and Your staff, they comfort me. You prepare a table before me in the presence of my enemies" (Psalm 23:4,5).

From these scriptures it is obvious that God wants and expects us to gain victories over our enemy, Satan, all the time. God has provided this for us through the unquestioned victory of Jesus over all the powers of darkness. If we fail to enter into the victory Jesus has provided for us we will not be able to live at the higher level of effective witness God has planned for us. We must follow the example set for us by Jesus and pray for unity of the bride of Christ.

My theme verse is:

"I do not pray for these alone, but also for those who will believe in Me through their word; _that they all may be one_, as You, Father, are in Me, and I in You; that they also may be one in Us, that the world may believe that You sent Me" (John 17:20,21, emphasis mine).

I came to America as an immigrant from England in 1963 and became a naturalized US citizen in 1982 (still holding dual nationality). For over 50 years I have seen the deterioration of this country and have a passionate desire to see both American and English Christians living in revival relationship with their Lord—and beyond this, for such to be the experiential life of Christians everywhere. The Church of Jesus Christ will not produce the effectiveness she should have in witness to the world without the life-giving inspiring energy of individual and corporate spiritual awakenings. The history of the Church clearly demonstrates this to be true. In fact, I believe we are fast losing the America we have known if we sit back in our comfortable recliners and do nothing about our desperate need for the Church to be all God has planned for her. We are to be the army of the Holy Spirit, and to be empowered with effective witness to the world around us.

As God's people, we must show that we are serious by seeking the Lord with passionate intercession for the power of the Gospel to be witnessed through all of us who claim the name of Jesus Christ. In other words, we urgently need to be actively and individually living revived, passionate, and powerful Christian witnesses as evidenced through our daily lives. After moving to America from England I have watched over the years with great concern the spiritual deterioration along with the advance of secularism taking place in both countries with which I have personal ties.

While other areas of the world are seeing enthusiastic Christians enjoying great moves of God, even while suffering severe persecution, there has in general been a seeming reluctance in America to seek God with all earnestness. There is an urgent need for Christians to seek God through prayer and fasting for the Church to become all we should be in unity as His witnesses within our own culture. Satan has hoodwinked the Church to relegate prayer accompanied with fasting as something Christians can decide for themselves to include as part of their devotional life, or not. But fasting is not optional for the Christian since Jesus obviously expected His followers to observe this self-humbling practice as part of their prayer life. In Matthew 6:16-18 Jesus says **"When you fast,"** not, "If you fast." Of course, we all realize that there may be physical conditions which make it impossible for some people to fast. On this important subject I have included Chapter 20, titled: *The Answer: Prayer and Fasting.*

However, a lack of such earnestness in seeking God in the ways He has prescribed is especially noticeable in Western Europe, England and the United States. Church attendance, especially among the younger generation, has been on the decrease for many years in spite of the springing up of mega churches that exist in several of our larger cities.

Unfortunately, Christians are often more eager to fight among themselves over doctrine rather than pray for one another. Some time ago a Christian whom I had met sent me a book attempting to convince me of a specific tenet of his denomination's doctrines. I wrote a letter back to him in a spirit of Christian love with a question:

"Could it be that love for your _______ denominational doctrine is causing you to sin without realizing it?"

Based on New Testament teachings I believe this would be the sin of causing *unnecessary division in the body of Christ!* Surely this is something of serious concern in the eyes of God as we will see in the following chapters showing the heart of our Lord through the prayer of Jesus in John 17. I have observed that good Christians can fall into the trap of trying to press a particular denominational doctrine upon others, when in the understanding of many biblical scholars the doctrine they believe may actually be questionable, exaggerated, or out of proportion when compared with the whole counsel of God's Word. It is as though a mindset of self-deception somehow gains a foothold in the minds of such people, and without really understanding the implications of what they are doing they feel compelled to try and impose a certain doctrinal belief upon others (they may honestly feel they are serving God in doing so). Such can sadly result in issues like the ones James referred to when he wrote, **"Where do wars and fights come from among you?"** (James 3:1). Note that James said, **"among you,"** meaning those recognized as professed Christians.

Now when it comes to considering specific doctrinal viewpoints, which is one thing, it is quite a different matter when seeking to obey the clear general command of Jesus to be passionate witnesses for Him by sharing the truth of the Gospel with the unsaved (Acts 1:8). Surely all true Christians regardless of denominational affiliation would accept this exhortation from Jesus without question or debate. After all, we are clearly commanded to **"Go therefore and make disciples of all the nations"** (Matthew 28:19). But when one Christian wants another to believe exactly the same way he or she has chosen to believe about a certain denominational dogma and doctrine, it can do more harm than good.

We cannot take the time or space in this writing to remind ourselves of the disastrous events which took place both before and after the Protestant Reformation involving professed Christians literally guilty of murdering one another. Yes, history clearly and sadly shows that the enemy, Satan, can wreak havoc among God's people if they do not stay close to God in personal commitment and intimate relationship. Therefore, we should be very sensitive to any trend that appears to generate division and separation in the body of Christ.

In fact, as suggested by the question above, doing so may lead to sin in the eyes of God because it can produce exactly what God does not want: *unnecessary division in the body of Christ, and a grieving of the Holy Spirit*. Even if some may think sin is too strong a word in this case, it would surely be agreed among Christians that unnecessary division in the Church is grieving to the Holy Spirit, and this is definitely something to be avoided. The Apostle Paul writes:

"And do not grieve the Holy Spirit of God, by whom you were sealed for the day of redemption" (Ephesians 4:30).

In this book you will find the heart of God's desire for His people as clearly revealed in His Word, and particularly by the prayer and words of Jesus Christ Himself in John's Gospel chapter 17. God's desire is that the body of Christ, the Church, be truly representative of a body in harmony with itself and in spiritual unity with Him. Just as we know a person's physical body only feels well when in general health and vitality, so the bride of Christ is able to operate with the full effectiveness God has planned for her only when all parts are in harmony and agreement with one another. Psalm 133 describes such a scenario beautifully:

"Behold, how good and how pleasant *it is* for brethren to dwell together in unity! *It is* **like the precious oil upon the head, running down on the beard, the beard of Aaron, running down on the edge of his garments.** *It is* **like the dew of Hermon, descending upon the mountains of Zion; for there the Lord commanded the blessing—life for evermore."**

Can you catch this vision for true followers of Christ in America? Do current conditions in our country tend to cause doubt that a turn-around for God is possible? Here is a significant quote from Dr. Jim Denison's daily column:

> "I am absolutely convinced that America's moral and spiritual future rests with America's Christians. My reason is emphatically not because we are better than anyone else or more deserving of God's favor.

It is because a lost person "does not accept the things of the Spirit of God, for they are folly to him, and he is not able to understand them because they are spiritually discerned" (1 Corinthians 2:14). God speaks his life-changing word to those who can receive and share it. We are our nation's only salt and light (Matthew 5:13-16).
That's why it is imperative that we meet with our Lord every day; that we seek his word for us from Scripture, prayer, and worship; that we follow [King] David's example by giving every challenge we face to our Father in prayer. He has a new word for each new day." (comments@denisonforum.org accessed 9-27-2018)

I pray that each of you who takes the time and effort to read this book will receive encouragement to pursue your relationship with God, increase your faith, and pray for America, England, and all God's people everywhere. As each of us is faithful to do this I believe we can increasingly see the fruitfulness of His presence working from within us to positively affect the lives of those around us.

I pray that the Lord will speak to you through this book according to your individual need, and that with God's help we can get to the stage of maturity where we can identify with the Apostle Paul who wrote:

"For if we live, we live to the Lord; and if we die, we die to the Lord. Therefore, whether we live or die, we are the Lord's" (Romans 14:8).

God bless you. Rod Butterworth

Spiritual Acknowledgements

Dear Lord, I thank you for:

Abel, Enoch, Noah, Abraham, Joseph, Moses, Isaiah, Daniel, Ezekiel, Joel, Matthew, Mark, Luke, Peter, John, Paul, Ignatius, Clement, Polycarp, Eusebius, Augustine, Calvin, Arminius, Wycliffe, Tyndale, Luther, Knox, Whitfield, Edwards, J. Wesley, E. Roberts, D. Campbell, Jeffries, Finney, Torrey, Spurgeon, Moody, Seymour, Booth, Parham, Hodge, McPherson, Woodworth-Etter, Murray, Bounds, Meyer, Henry, Howells, Lake, Lockyer, Graham, Kulman, Hagin, Shakarian, Wigglesworth, O. Roberts, McDowell, Sproul, MacArthur, Pawson, M. Brown, and many others too numerous to name.

Special thanks to Mary Schlegel for her valuable help with editorial proofreading.

But supremely and above all, I thank God my Heavenly Father, Jesus my Lord and Savior, and Holy Spirit my Strength, Power and Guide.

Chapter 1
The World is Watching

Do I really care whether I am in unity with other Christians? If I am honest with myself, could it just be my immediate family and circle of friends that I am mainly concerned be in harmony with one another? Do I enjoy the fellowship of the Christians in my own church, but have no passion or burden that churches in general would present a unified oneness to the unsaved world? Yes, the world is watching, and in particular is watching America!

If our mindset is such that we are not really concerned with the lack of unity among Christians, we are surely in a state of understanding that is far from agreement with the scripturally revealed desires of God. We would be seeing the Church from a very narrow perspective compared to the vision and desire God has for His people. God is love (1 John 4:8), and He desires His love to be the kind of love with which we as the Church love one another. In fact, God sets a high standard for His Church and expects to find His bride ready and glorious in love and holiness when He comes for her. Could it be that the personal individual relationship of Christians to God through prayer and His Word is lacking? Could it also be a reason for apathy on this eternally relevant issue? Ephesians 5:27 says:

"Husbands, love your wives, just as Christ also loved the church and gave Himself for her, that He might sanctify and cleanse her with the washing of water by the word, that He might present her to himself a glorious church, not having spot of wrinkle or any such thing, but that she should be holy and without blemish."

How can we be a **"glorious church"** in America when we are plagued with so many denominational divisions? Are we not *spotted* and *wrinkled*? However, we can start by recognizing and believing the vital spiritual truth that we are already one in Him as true believers, and therefore *should* be able to demonstrate a supernatural oneness for the world around us to observe. We should never forget the purpose of the Church from God's point of view, which is to be a living witness of His presence within His people in order to reach out with His love and Holy-Spirit power for the salvation of the lost. Jesus said that our oneness should be demonstrated **"that the world may believe"** (John 17:21). But if the unsaved world only observes the Church failing to express love for one another, they will continue to doubt the Church has any relevance, value, or meaning for their personal lives.

Falcons, Bulldogs, Vikings, Hornets, Yellow Jackets, Tigers, Razorbacks, Bears, Bobcats, Eagles, Cardinals, Giants, Cowboys, and Pirates! What do these words represent? They are identifying labels (in America) given to teams that compete in sporting events.

Question: Do some churches actually compete with one another in order to have more attendees, more money for expansion, and boast about being the biggest and most effective church in town? We hope not, but if such an attitude exists it surely contributes to unnecessary division, and therefore cannot be pleasing to God.

In the scripture mentioned above from Ephesians 5:27, it reminds us that Christ sacrificed His life for the Church in order that He might **"sanctify and cleanse her with the washing of water by the word."** Simply put, the Church needs to be sanctified and cleansed from all that is unholy through the penetrating conviction, workings, and impact of the Holy Spirit and the Word of God. God clearly commands His Church to be holy. Peter wrote:

"But as He who called you is holy, you also be holy in all your conduct [manner of living], **because it is written, 'Be holy, for I am holy' "** (1 Peter 1:15,16).

But this can only be accomplished in individual lives through the continual dynamic indwelling presence of the Lord by the Holy Spirit. The Bible is powerful in and of itself, and will be highly effective in our lives through **"the washing of water by the word"** if applied in faith accompanied with the genuine motive of a desire to please God. No psychologist can expose the deepest desires and motives of the human heart to the depth and extent the Word of God does when applied by the Holy Spirit.

"For the word of God is living and powerful, and sharper than any two-edged sword, piercing even to the division of soul and spirit, and of joints and marrow, and is a discerner of the thoughts and intents of the heart" (Hebrews 4:12).

And Jesus said:

"It is the Spirit who gives life; the flesh profits nothing. The words that I speak to you are spirit, and they are life" (John 6:63).

Notice, **"The words that I speak to you...."** The words Jesus spoke two thousand years ago are not only written in the Bible with ink on paper, but they are alive with meaning and purpose when proclaimed with the anointing of the Holy Spirit as demonstrated on the Day of Pentecost (Acts 2). The Spirit and the Word are as one when working together to reach into the heart and soul of individuals with the truth.

Question: Is the Church actively showing willingness to take the Bible seriously when it comes to God's desire for unity based on true genuine love? We certainly should be if we want to accomplish that which is pleasing to God. When the Church as a whole is not united in service to the Lord, it is surely lacking power that would be present if we were more openly joined together in oneness.

Jesus was faced with the challenge of encouraging true unity to develop among the small group of disciples He had surrounded himself with, and with whom He planned to be His instruments to turn the world **"upside down"** (Acts 17:6). The disciples were not highly educated, and would have been looked upon by the Jewish elite as rather simple and unimportant to the advancement of their society. Neither would they easily nor naturally be considered a promising group that would automatically be melded together in unity, agreement, and love for each other. In fact, they sometimes demonstrated heated disagreement and dislike for one another. For example:

"And when the ten [disciples] **heard** *it* **they were greatly displeased with the two brothers"** (Matthew 20:24). Due to their political thinking, James and John came to Jesus with their mother to ask if they could be the ones to sit on either side of Him when He came into His kingdom (they were thinking of a political kingdom without Roman oppression). This did not go over well with the other disciples at all. They were **"greatly displeased"** and must have expressed their displeasure in strong, condemning words. How sad it is when Christians use harsh words of disagreement in speaking to one another. This is often over matters which could be resolved with respect and love if the wisdom of the Holy Spirit was earnestly sought and applied. He would be only too willing to impart His wise direction if sought sincerely. Some of us know from experience how Church board meetings can be traditionally notorious for lack of unity and agreement—even in matters concerning the color and design of carpeting!

In Jesus' wonderfully revealing prayer recorded in John 17 we see His deep concern for the disciples to be united as one. He prayed, **"I pray for them. I do not pray for the world but for those whom You have given Me, for they are Yours"** (John 17:9). It may be a surprise to be reminded by this portion of Jesus' prayer that He did not pray for the unbelieving world. It was more important for Him to pray for His disciples because they were the ones who were going to be His instruments to reach the lost secular world. They were specially chosen to be His emissaries, with their lives and testimonies committed to demonstrating God's presence and power in order to impact the world with the Gospel. And so we see that the baton of witness has been handed down through the centuries to each generation of Christians—including us.

This means that all twenty-first-century Christians have the responsibility of proclaiming the truth of the Gospel with love. Each of us is responsible individually, and the Church corporately, to be true disciples and ambassadors for spreading the Gospel truths to the world around us. But how successful has our modern-day witness been in Western Europe and American populations?

Is our twenty-first-century culture, particularly in countries like America and England, becoming more Christian or less Christian? We all know the sad and alarming answer. Some have even used the term *post Christian* to identify the current situation. Evil is increasing exponentially as reported by the daily news. The spiritual powers of darkness are doing their best to push true Christianity out of public awareness and marginalize the Bible and all it stands for as irrelevant to modern society. But the Bible is absolutely prophetically right when it gives vivid descriptions of the unholy depths to which sin can bring to humankind. For example,

"But evil men and impostors will grow worse and worse, deceiving and being deceived" (2 Timothy 3:13).

Also:

"And even as they did not like to retain God in *their* **knowledge, God gave them over to a debased mind, to do those things which are not fitting; being filled with all unrighteousness, sexual immorality, wickedness, covetousness, maliciousness; full of envy, murder, strife, deceit, evil-mindedness;** *they* **are whisperers, backbiters, haters of God, violent, proud, boasters, inventors of evil things, disobedient to parents, undiscerning, untrustworthy, unloving, unforgiving, unmerciful"** (Romans 1:28-31).

And:

"But know this, that in the last days perilous times will come: For men will be lovers of themselves, lovers of money, boasters, proud, blasphemers, disobedient to parents, unthankful, unholy, unloving, unforgiving slanderers, without self-control, brutal, despisers of good, traitors, headstrong, haughty, lovers of pleasure rather than lovers of God, having a form of godliness but denying its power" (2 Timothy 3:1-5).

Unfortunately, these scriptures are so descriptive of life today. Just as it was in the early days of Christianity and in some areas of the world arguably worse, Christians are faced with challenges that would leave us despairing if it were not for the assurance received from God's promise to be a very present help for us in our daily lives. The writer of Hebrews says:

"For He Himself has said, *'I will never leave you nor forsake you.'* **So we may boldly say:** *'The Lord is my helper; I will not fear. What can man do to me?'* **"** (Hebrews 13:5,6).

By faith we have all the resources of His abiding presence available within us. Our lives should demonstrate to the watching world around us that we have something within us (Someone), who enables us to face all the challenges of life with courage, peace, and joy.

We also have an enemy who delights in spawning conflict, disagreement, and disharmony among Christians in his ongoing rebellion against God. It is sad and detrimental to the cause of the Gospel if the unsaved world perceives the various segments of the Church as a disagreeable, confused, segregated, unhappy group of people who cannot get along with one another—thank God there are exceptions). While we think about this sad state of affairs, it is important to remember always the bigger picture of God's plan for His Church.

We should never lose sight of the main purpose, which is to save souls and spread the love of God throughout the world by means of proclaiming the Gospel. In order to do this with spiritual strength received from the Holy Spirit, resulting in fruitfulness, we, the Church, should have our corporate house in order and in readiness to engage the forces of darkness. After all, we should remember that we are blessed to be children of the most high and only God, and He is our ever-present help.

We have to ask ourselves if we are ready and willing to engage the enemy in the spiritual warfare with the right weapons God has provided for us. Satan and his minions of seducing spirits will not stand idly by while the proclaiming of the Word of God in Holy-Spirit power is threatening their evil kingdom. We certainly must be serious about taking the Apostle Paul's exhortation to avail ourselves of the spiritual armor God provides for us, both as individuals and as the corporate Church. We are told to:

"Put on the whole armor of God, that you may be able to stand against the wiles of the devil. For we do not wrestle against flesh and blood, but against principalities, against powers, against the rulers of the darkness of this age, against

spiritual *hosts* of wickedness in the heavenly *places.* **Therefore, take up the whole armor of God, that you may be able to withstand in the evil day, and having done all, to stand"** (Ephesians 6:11-13).

Yes, it is always important for us to remember we are not fighting against human personalities, but against the evil entities and influences working from within and behind those who are engaged in evil lifestyles and acts. At the same time, we are to love with the love of God, and such love is a power that can conquer all. As we obey our Lord and go forth into the arena of spiritual warfare knowing we are being watched by our Lord, Satan, and the world, we must take our stand in faith on the promises in the Word that are there for us to apply and be victorious by faith. Psalm 56:9-11 reads:

"In the day I cry to You, then my enemies will turn back; this I know, that God is for me. In God whose word I praise, in the Lord whose word I praise, in God I trust, I will not fear; what can man do to me?"

And, Psalm 18:1-3:

"I will love You, O Lord, my strength. The Lord is my rock and my fortress and my deliverer; My God, my strength, in whom I will trust; My shield and the horn of my salvation, my stronghold. I will call upon the Lord, *who is worthy* to be praised; So shall I be saved from my enemies."

The Church of Jesus Christ is not called to shrink back for fear of what the enemy may want to do. We are not to retreat and hide in the shadows of anonymity in order to avoid the scandal of the absolute necessity to proclaim the message of the cross. Jesus nakedly exposed Himself under His Father's leading to the worst that the enemy could do, and the result was salvation for all who choose to believe. We, and I include myself, must be willing to live daily in the reality of Paul's challenging exhortation to believers as found in Romans 12:1,2 which reads:

"I beseech [Gr. *Parakaleo*—to seriously urge] **you therefore, brethren, by the mercies of God, that you present your bodies a living sacrifice, holy, acceptable to God, *which is* your reasonable service. And do not be conformed to this world, but be transformed by the renewing of your mind, that you may prove what *is* that good and acceptable and perfect will of God."**

Such is the only way for our lives as individual Christians to glorify God and produce fruitfulness. It is only in this short earthly life we have the opportunity to obey God and experience the blessedness of being His servants. We should consider it the highest privilege and joy to identify with the Apostle Paul who referred to himself as **"Paul, a bondservant of Jesus Christ"** (Romans 1:1). In the following chapters we will see how to proceed by absorbing the truths found in the wonderful prayer of Jesus found in the Gospel of John chapter 17.

Chapter 2
Glorify to Glorify
John 17:1

"Jesus spoke these words, lifted up His eyes to heaven, and said: 'Father, the hour has come. Glorify Your Son, that Your Son also may glorify You.'"

Merriam Webster's Collegiate Dictionary, Eleventh Edition under the heading "glorify" reads: "to make glorious by bestowing honor, praise, and admiration; to elevate to celestial glory." This prayer prayed by Jesus while still in an unglorified, natural, physical body during the three years of His ministry, was prayed with perfect faith in His relationship with the Father. It was a petition that we would probably think not necessary for Jesus to pray. Our thinking would most likely be along the line that Jesus was already glorious as the sinless Son of God.

But Jesus prayed this prayer because the answer to it would be accomplished through what was about to happen in just a few short hours. The extreme personal sacrifice He was volitionally submitting Himself to undergo by a cruel crucifixion was the means through which He would afterward be glorified. The **"hour"** had come, and Jesus needed all the faith and assurance of His relationship with the Father in order to continue with a courage and commitment beyond anything we have observed in examples of sacrificial living in others. This was a prayer looking beyond the crucifixion and resurrection to the reality of a complete victory over the world, the flesh, and the devil, not only for Him but for all who would believe in Him.

Jesus had to overcome and maintain victory over all the temptations and tests that came to Him and to every human being during our earthly lives. He did this in a world that was then, and still is today, extremely wicked and full of sinful allurements causing many to succumb to unrighteousness. This is His plan for us, that we should be righteous and holy by faith in His holy presence within us. Jesus lived a sinless life. In Revelation 3:21 Jesus said:

"To him who overcomes I will grant to sit with Me on My throne, as I also overcame and sat down with My Father on His throne."

Do we think it was easy for Jesus to *overcome* because He was the Son of God? No, of course it wasn't easy. The Bible records of Jesus **"For in that He Himself has suffered, being tempted, He is able to aid those who are tempted"** (Hebrews 2:18). And, **"For we do not have a High Priest who cannot sympathize with our weaknesses, but was in all *points* tempted as *we are,* yet without sin"** (Hebrews 4:15).

There had to be suffering before glorification. Jesus paved the way for us to follow in His footsteps. He is our example to encourage us as we continue upward on our individual journeys of faith and maturity in Him. The world doesn't like the cross and all it stands for because it reminds them of Jesus. Secular groups such as the Freedom From Religion Foundation have it as one of their aims to have all visible crosses removed from public view. The cross brings to mind the tortuous, bloody, cruel dehumanization of individuals who are put to death by this method. But Jesus suffered such because of His love for the Father and for those whom the Father had given Him, and would give Him in the future—let us remember this includes us today!

What amazing submission to the Father we see in Jesus as He faced the most traumatic time of suffering not equaled by any other individual in the history of the world. It is natural for humans to avoid suffering, but Jesus was willing to embrace the cross.

He knew it was the right thing to do for the future of the kingdom of God and all who would be privileged to be a part of His eternal kingdom. In other words, He did it for the new covenant Church of the New Testament—hopefully, the ones you and I are part of.

We need to remember that the suffering of Jesus on the cross was more than physical, as horrendous as that was in and of itself, which others besides Jesus have experienced. But there is something else that makes His sacrifice supremely more significant and above all others. Since the beginning of the world when physical death entered the scene, the Scriptures make plain that innocent blood was required by God to pave the way for forgiveness of sin. In Genesis 3:7,21 we read:

"They [Adam and Eve] **sewed fig leaves together and made themselves coverings . . . Also for Adam and his wife, the Lord God made tunics of skin, and clothed them."**

This is the first physical death mentioned in Scripture. Whatever the kind of animal God sacrificed to clothe Adam and Eve (possibly a lamb which ties in with Jesus being referred to in Revelation 13:8 as **"...the Lamb slain from the foundation of the world"**), it was obviously a type and symbol of the requirement for a perfect, sinless blood sacrifice to provide covering and forgiveness of sins. The skins God prepared may have still had fresh blood on them as Adam and Eve were covered with them. Today, the perfect blood sacrifice of Jesus on the cross is still viable and able to freshly forgive the sins of those who sincerely repent. This is why the sacrifice of Jesus was different. It was because He was bearing the load and sins of all humanity as the perfect and sinless Lamb of God.

Why did Jesus ask the Father to glorify Him? Because by being glorified with complete victory over the world, the flesh, and the devil, He would become the Savior of God's creation for all who would believe. The only hope for a sinful wicked world was for God's righteous justice to be appeased. If it were not for this sublime act carried out by Jesus two thousand years ago, neither the Old Testament saints nor New Testament believers would have any hope of everlasting bliss in eternal ages to come.

How does this knowledge affect us today as twenty-first-century Christians? We should realize like Jesus that we all have a prayer to pray. Jesus prayed that His life would glorify the Father, and I believe we are to follow His example. In other words, we should be praying something like this: "Father God and our Lord Jesus Christ, please glorify my life with the power of your presence so that I will bring glory and honor to You and Your name."

Could there be any greater purpose in life than directing praise and glory to the Father who loved us so much that He gave Jesus to us as our perfect Redeemer? We have the opportunity to do exactly this if we will apply ourselves with willing obedience as His servants. From the very beginning of creation when God gave Adam and Eve the test in the garden, we understand His desire is for there to be a people with whom He shares a loving relationship. This is why He created us.

In our finite minds it is difficult if not impossible to comprehend the absolute holiness and justice of a perfect God. We see and hear things happening on Earth that are so terrible and unholy, we can become desensitized to evil and despair of any hope of living a life that is pleasing to such a God. But here is the good news: God has provided a way for us to come into relationship with Him without feelings of complete unworthiness. Yes, we know we are certainly unworthy in and of ourselves, but the amazing biblical truth is that God has arranged a perfect way in which we can expect a close intimate relationship with Him if we fulfill His conditions. Yes, there are always conditions, just as we see in the Garden of Eden. As Adam and Eve were wrapped in the animal skins to hide their unworthiness, so we can be spiritually covered by the blood of our sinless Savior and are thus forgiven, covered, protected, and no longer under condemnation for our past sins. Jesus becomes our spiritual covering of righteousness. The Apostle wrote of this amazing gift from God in Jesus:

"But of Him you are in Christ Jesus, who became for us wisdom from God—and righteousness and sanctification and redemption" (1 Corinthians 1:30).

We can never be a sacrifice for our own sins, but like Jesus we can and should be willing to sacrifice our wills to the will of the Father. In fact, as mentioned before, we are exhorted by the Apostle Paul with these words:

"I beseech you therefore, brethren, by the mercies of God, that you present your bodies a living sacrifice, holy, acceptable to God, *which* is your reasonable service" (Romans 12:1).

Our physical lives are very precious to us. If we have physical problems with our bodies we would certainly wish for restoration and healing, and will do everything possible to enhance our health. If we are wise we will always look for ways and methods to preserve our bodies and prevent pain and discomfort. But, if we are not careful we can be so enamored by our bodies if they happen to be handsome and beautiful (as many are), that we can develop the wrong understanding to the extent that we believe we own our bodies to the exclusion of God. We need to let the Holy Spirit remind us:

"Or do you not know that your body is the temple of the Holy Spirit *who is* in you, whom you have from God, and you are not your own? For you were bought at a price; therefore glorify God in your body and in your spirit, which are God's" (1 Corinthians 6:19,20).

How blind are some who believe they have the right to do with their bodies whatever they please! The awful example of this thinking is the woman who believes she can have the new life developing within her murdered by abortion for the sake of personal convenience. No, we have been **"bought at a price"** and the sinful desecration of our physical bodies is a crime with eternal consequences. Notice also in the scripture above that as Christians we are expected to **"glorify God"** through our whole beings, body and spirit/soul.

As Jesus submitted His will to the will of the Father, so we need to do the same. It is not complicated, but simply a question of whether or not we are willing to obey God. Therefore, the literal presenting of our physical lives to God's service is a witness of our submission to let God be God. In this way our lives will bring glory to God, and by glorifying Him we will be blessed and raised to ever increasing levels of intimate relationship with Him. Paul wrote:

"But we all, with unveiled face, beholding as in a mirror the glory of the Lord, are being transformed into the same image from glory to glory, just as by the Spirit of the Lord" (2 Corinthians 3:18).

But we are the ones who have to do the **"beholding."** This word means to reflect as when using a mirror. Physically, the only way to see our reflection is by positioning ourselves close to the mirror. If we are to reflect the glory of our Lord we must maintain an intimate face-to-face relationship with Him as Jesus did with the Father. How do we do this? By following the example of Jesus through time spent developing and maintaining such a relationship. In other words, by making personal time and circumstances bow to regular prayer and meditation times in the Word of God each day.

Our lives and witness cannot give out or project the glory of God until we are actually receiving such glory. Once again, Jesus is the perfect example, and this is why He requested the Father's glory for Himself. It was for the reciprocal purpose of glorifying the Father.

Our daily Christian experience should never become so predictable and routine that we lose the excitement of increasing in our knowledge and intimacy with the Lord. The scripture above says there should be a continuous process of being **"transformed"** into the image or likeness of our Lord. This is why the Apostle Paul wrote these passionate words:

"That I may know Him and the power of His resurrection, and the fellowship of His sufferings, being conformed to His death" (Philippians 3:10).

If we really come to know Him intimately we can expect the glory of His presence to be revealed through our desires, thoughts, words, and actions. In this way our lives will bring glory to God, the One who has made all this possible. We *can* be vessels that contribute to the unity of oneness that Jesus prays for all of us to become as believers.

Do you want your life to bring glory to God? You know what you must do. Pray, seek the Lord, and believe. Why not start right now?

Chapter 3
Recognizing the Head
John 17:2

"As You have given Him authority over all flesh, that He should give eternal life to as many as You have given Him."

How foolish it is for people not to recognize and respect those who have legitimate authority over them. Young children are expected to abide by the authority of their parents as they grow up and mature. Employees are expected to fulfill the requirements of their jobs by doing a good day's work for their employers. But unfortunately, we observe that many act foolishly by deciding to resist those in authority over them—often over unnecessary disagreement about minor issues. Because the Apostle Paul knew very well the tendency of sinful people to resent any authority over them, he wrote:

"Let every soul be subject to the governing authorities. For there is no authority except from God, and the authorities that exist are appointed by God. Therefore whoever resists the authority resists the ordinance of God, and those who resist will bring judgment on themselves" (Romans 13:1,2).

If we recognize the need to give respect to those in authority over us at the human level, how much more should we honor our Creator to whom we owe our lives and existence? The Father has given Jesus **"authority over all flesh"** and the time will come when the whole of creation will recognize this. Paul wrote:

"Therefore God also has highly exalted Him and given Him the name which is above every name, that at the name of Jesus every knee

should bow, of those in heaven, and of those on earth, and of those under the earth, and *that* every tongue should confess that Jesus Christ *is* Lord, to the glory of God the Father"** (Philippians 2:9-11).

But until that time there are multitudes that do not look to Jesus as an authority in their lives. They are walking in spiritual darkness and lack understanding for the reason of their existence. Jesus is the focal point of all history, and acceptance or rejection of Him for who He is decides the eternal destiny of every human being. This life is a testing ground for all of us, and in a similar way to the God-ordained test Adam and Eve faced in the garden, our eternal future is determined by our relationship to Jesus Christ. After Jesus had demonstrated His power over death by raising His earthly body from the dead, Matthew records Him saying, **"All authority has been given to Me in heaven and on earth"** (Matthew 28:18).

What should be our relationship with Jesus concerning the Church and our involvement as part of the body of Christ? First of all we must recognize the Church's head. Paul makes this clear when he writes:

"And He [the Father] **put all *things* under His** [Jesus'] **feet, and gave Him *to be* head over all *things* to the church, which is His body, the fullness of Him who fills all in all"** (Ephesians 1:22,23).

Jesus is the head of His Church. It is because of His presence in each individual that it is possible for the Church to be powerful in unity of oneness. If we are filled with the Spirit, we are filled with the abiding indwelling presence of Jesus. It may sound strange to some to put it this way, but Jesus earned the right to be head of the Church. Think of His suffering in the Garden of Gethsemane when He prayed with agonizing passion:

"My soul is exceedingly sorrowful, even to death. Stay here and watch with Me. He went a little farther and fell on His face, and prayed, saying, 'O My Father, if it is possible, let this cup pass from Me; nevertheless, not as I will, but as You *will*' " (Matthew 26:38,39).

Many Christians, including myself, would look upon this experience of Jesus in the garden as demonstrating the most important and dramatic prayer in all of the Bible and history. Everything depended upon Jesus' submission to the Father and willingness to go to the cross. He was willing to suffer in anticipation of the joy that was going to follow afterwards. Ever since God created man in the Garden of Eden, He has been looking for a people He could call His own—a people who would be joined together in loving unity with Him and with each other. His desire is, **"That He might present her to himself a glorious church, not having spot or wrinkle or any such thing, but that she should be holy and without blemish"** (Ephesians 5:27).

We must remain low to be high! In other words, we should humbly accept God's leading and direction. We should be humble and willing to fit in where God wants us to be as individual and unique members of His spiritual body. Just as people in the military need to recognize and obey their superiors in rank, so we as Christians should submit under God to those He has put over our lives in positions of leadership. The Apostle Paul speaks of this in Ephesians 4:11-13:

"And He Himself gave some *to be* apostles, some prophets, some evangelists, and some pastors and teachers, for the equipping of the saints for the work of ministry, for the edifying of the body of Christ, till we all come to the unity of the faith and of the knowledge of the Son of God, to a perfect man, to the measure of the stature of the fullness of Christ."

Obviously, God knows exactly how He wants His Church to grow and impact those who do not yet know Him. We should always remember God's supreme purpose as seen in John 3:16, that **"...whoever believes in Him should not perish but have everlasting life."** He wants as many people as possible to enter into the life of salvation that leads to eternal life. His plan is for there to be a glorious company of united believers who will together experience the promised future new heavens and new earth. If each of us will sincerely and humbly seek God for His leading as to where we fit in as members of His Church, we will find our lives being fruitful for the advancement of the Kingdom of God. Paul uses the human body as an illustration of the cohesiveness and cooperation needed for the successful ministry of the body of Christ. The various gifts of the Holy Spirit to the Church should work together in beautiful harmony. He wrote:

"There are diversities of gifts, but the same Spirit...For in fact the body is not one member but many. If the foot should say, 'Because I am not a hand, I am not of the body,' is it therefore not of the body? And if the ear should say, 'Because I am not an eye, I am not of the body,' is it therefore not of the body?...And if they *were* all one member, where *would* the body be? But now indeed *there are* many members, yet one body" (1 Corinthians 12:4,14-16,19,20).

It is easy to become excited about what our individual parts are to be in our service to the Lord, and we must be careful not to run ahead of God in our honest zeal to please. This is why it is always so crucial and important to recognize Jesus as the absolute Head of His Church. He knows exactly where each of us should fit in according to His perfect plan and purpose. As His servants and humbling ourselves in teachable positions before Him we should always be ready to pray a prayer like this one from Psalm 25:4,5:

"Show me Your ways, O Lord; Teach me Your paths. Lead me in Your truth and teach me, for You *are* the God of my salvation; On You I wait all the day."

And to remember promises like this one:

"I will instruct you and teach you in the way you should go; I will guide you with My eye" (Psalm 32:8).

Yet, what do we observe happening in many of today's churches? We see all kinds of activities and methods of *doing church work* that very often stem from secular and worldly ideas. For example, churches may providing classes on counseling that use secular psychology without a biblical foundation. Since we are serving the Lord of all creation, we should come before Him in humble submission and prayerfully request His leading and direction which He has already promised to give us. As true believers we are blessed with the awesome reality of Christ's presence resident within us by the Holy Spirit Jesus promised for all who remain in Him. He enlightens us of this truth through the pen of John when He said:

"However, when He, the Spirit of truth, has come, He will guide you into all truth; for He will not speak on His own *authority,* but whatever He hears He will speak; and He will tell you things to come" (John 16:13).

What amazing spiritual resources God has provided for us! The Holy Spirit **"hears"** from God the Father and the Son, and then brings what He hears to us. But we have to ask ourselves: Are we hearing what He is speaking to us? If all of us individually follow the plan for His Church with a willingness to be united in oneness as we serve, the impact on our communities will be effective and powerful. Jesus reminds us that as His Church we are supposed to be the influence that affects those around us positively for good and for God's purposes, rather than the prevalent secular influences negatively affecting our communities. He said:

"**You are the salt of the earth; but if the salt loses its flavor, how shall it be seasoned? It is then good for nothing but to be thrown out and trampled underfoot by men. You are the light of the world. A city that is set on a hill cannot be hidden. Nor do they light a lamp and put it under a basket, but on a lampstand, and it gives light to all** *who are* **in the house. Let your light shine before men, that they may see your good works and glorify your Father in heaven**" (Matthew 5:13-16).

In our key verse for this chapter Jesus is spoken of as the giver of eternal life to those whom the Father has given Him, "**...that He should give eternal life to as many as You have given Him.**" Who are the ones the Father gives Him? Once again from John chapter 3 we see that they are those who actively *believe.* Notice from the following well-known passage of Scripture that the plural **"believes"** is recorded three times in the Greek New Testament manuscripts in the *present continuous sense.*

"**And as Moses lifted up the serpent in the wilderness, even so must the Son of Man be lifted up, that whoever** *believes* **in Him should not perish but have everlasting life. For God so loved the world that He gave His only begotten Son, that whoever** *believes* **in Him should not perish but have everlasting life...He who** *believes* **in Him is not condemned; but he who does not believe is condemned already, because he has not believed in the name of the only begotten Son of God**" (John 3:14-16,18, emphasis mine).

A person cannot receive the gift of eternal life until they *believe.* This is how our relationship with God begins and how it should continue. I know this will challenge some of particular theological persuasions, but throughout the New Testament it is clear that our continuing relationship with God depends upon an active, living, continuous faith which is itself supplied to us by the Holy Spirit if we are willing to present our lives to Him in humble obedience, submission, and service.

Sadly, there are teachings prevalent that have been with us for a long time, and continue to cause unnecessary division in the Church. One such well-known teaching is that God determined individual eternal destinies before creation as to who would be saved and who would be condemned. This does terrible injustice to the character and nature of God. It is pushing the biblical doctrine of the sovereignty of God beyond what the Scriptures reveal. With such in mind we could ask a question such as: Did God predetermine and preordain the holocaust? He certainly did not prevent it from happening. But let us be very careful how we answer a question like this. Again, we should beware of forcing the true concepts of grace and the sovereignty of God beyond what the Scriptures teach.

In relation to the word *believe* in John chapter three above, a helpful question for some to consider would be: Is it possible for a person to stop believing? If so, what would be the scriptural consequences? The Bible is what it is. We should be very careful to accept it just as God the Holy Spirit has given it to us. We were never meant to be like puppets on strings, which is why God allowed the test given to Adam and Eve in the Garden of Eden. In the introductory pages to this book I wrote:

"We should never bend the Scriptures to fit our theology.

We should bend our theology to fit the Scriptures."

Yes, to receive the gift of eternal life and to anticipate being in the presence of our Savior and Creator Jesus and God the Father forever, is something so wonderful to try and comprehend that it certainly seems beyond our finite understanding. Paul reminds us in 1 Corinthians 2:9 of what the Prophet Isaiah wrote:

"Eye has not seen not ear heard, nor have entered into the heart of man the things which God has prepared for those who love Him."

Then Paul adds:

"But God has revealed *them* to us through His Spirit. For the Spirit searches all things, yes, the deep things of God" (1 Corinthians 2:10).

So, according to Paul, if we have an intimate relationship with the Holy Spirit He will give us glimpses into that eternal realm. How can such real awareness come about in our own individual experiences? Only by living in close intimate relationship with our Lord through prayer and the application of His living Word. This takes time and discipline, and, of course, Jesus is our perfect example. May we continually offer praise and thanksgiving to God by fully recognizing His authority over His Church, and by rejoicing in the knowledge of the miraculous gift of eternal life. In other words, make sure you keep on believing.

Chapter 4
Knowing the Source of Life and Unity
John 17:3

"And this is eternal life, that they may know You, the only true God, and Jesus Christ whom You have sent."

Do you know God? Do you know Jesus Christ? Most Christians should be able to say they know God the Father and Jesus because they have experienced forgiveness of sins and the power to live a life of victory over sin. Transformed lives are certainly a credible witness to a power within a person enabling such change to take place. There are literally millions of examples of dramatic transformations that have occurred in the lives of people who, from all appearances, have seemed to be impossible cases for positive change.

But a more penetrating question would be: How *well* do we know God the Father and Jesus Christ the Son? In other words, to what degree or level of personal knowledge and intimacy can we say we know God? Jesus said in part of His prayer as quoted above, that the deeper reason we come into relationship with God at the time of our born-again experience is to *know* both Him and the Father. It is not just knowledge of coming into a saved relationship with God, but something with a much more profound meaning. The root Greek word used in this passage and many others is *ginosko*. It can be translated to include:

Taking in knowledge, to come to know, recognize, understand, or to understand completely...such knowledge is obtained, not by mere intellectual activity, but by operation of the Holy Spirit consequent upon acceptance of Christ...the verb is also used to convey the thought of connection or union, as between man and woman, Matt. 1:25; Luke 1:34 (W. E. Vine, *An Expository Dictionary of New Testament Words.* Fleming H. Revell Company, New Jersey, 1966 297-298).

Notice that Vine reminds us of the intimate relationship between a husband and wife, which should include a spiritual oneness that is much deeper than the merely physical aspects of marriage. Paul refers to this when writing about the relationship between husbands and wives in relation to the Church:

"Husbands, love your wives, just as Christ also loved the church and gave Himself for her...For we are members of His body, of His flesh and of His bones. *For this reason a man shall leave his father and mother and be joined to his wife, and the two shall become one flesh.'* This is a great mystery, but I speak concerning Christ and the church" (Ephesians 5:25,30-32).

Paul writes of Christian marriage and likens it to Christ and the Church as a **"great mystery."** There is a possibility of amazing spiritual oneness with Christ available for all Christians who will pursue such a relationship. Such spiritual union should be true both individually and corporately as the Church. How often do we think of ourselves in scriptural terms as **"members of His flesh and of His bones"?** This gets pretty personal doesn't it? Paul also gives us the foundation for really beginning to *know* God when he wrote concerning his own personal desire:

"And be found in Him, not having my own righteousness, which *is* from the law, but that which *is* through faith in Christ, the righteousness which is from God by faith; that I may know Him and the power of His resurrection, and the fellowship of His sufferings, being conformed to His death" (Philippians 3:9,10)

Paul relates the state of spiritual *righteousness* as a necessary step and precursor to being able to **"know Him."** This pictures a spiritual journey that all Christians should be passionately interested in—to be able to say that they truly **"know Him"** in spiritual depth. Is this what we see among the members of Christ's body as a whole in our twenty-first century Church? Sad to say, I don't think the evidence shows such to be the case. At this point I want the reader to know I am well aware of the fact that I dare not write such with any hint of condemnation, for I have to look at my own relationship with God first and see what might be lacking. I don't want to be guilty of trying to cast out the splinter when I may have a huge beam to deal with myself.

However, we do need to be sure we are in that holy state of righteousness before God if we are to move forward in our knowledge and relationship with Him. Paul tells us in the above scripture how this is accomplished. It is **"through faith in Christ, the righteousness which is from God by faith."** As I wrote earlier, the beginning, continuing and successful ending of our journey with God starts and ends with faith. If we exercise the faith given to us by God from the time of our conversion, we should be able to confess with confidence the words Paul wrote in 1 Corinthians 1:30,31:

"But of Him you are in Christ Jesus, who became for us wisdom from God—and righteousness and sanctification and redemption—as it is written, *'He who glories, let him glory in the Lord.'* "

Because of this scripture I often find myself personalizing this truth by praying:

"Thank you, Father, for making Jesus to be my wisdom, righteousness, sanctification and redemption, and all the glory is to you, my Lord."

Truly, God has supplied beyond bountifully all that we need in this life through Christ. Therefore, from the standpoint of the truth that we are covered by the righteousness of Christ, we should have confidence to pursue the intimate relationship with God we are talking about in this chapter. While all this is wonderful truth to consider, we are reminded through Scripture that God *expects us* to *actively involve ourselves* in the developing of our relationship with Him. Once again, Jesus is our perfect example. He has shown us the way to be close to Him and the Father. It is the same simple illustration that only by spending time with people is there the possibility of really becoming to know them. In my book *If My People,* I challenge all of us to prioritize the means and privilege of prayer God has provided for us. But at the same time I wonder how few of us in real-life daily experience actually avail ourselves of this means of grace to the extent we should. I wrote:

Imagine if Jesus were to actually physically appear to us—how would we explain our lack of prayer? Yes, such a thought suddenly elevates the matter of prayer to a much higher place of priority. So what can we do as Christians in order to get control of our lives and the use of our time? We can make a decision to subordinate mundane earthly activities to heavenly spiritual ones. In other words, we can put God first! This is something all of us are responsible for individually. Just as we are called to "humble ourselves" (1 Peter 5:6), so we are responsible to make decisions about the use of our limited time on this earth. During Jesus' earthly ministry we read: **"So He Himself often withdrew into the wilderness and prayed"** (Luke 5:16). **"He went out to the mountain to pray, and continued all night in prayer to God"** (Luke 6:12).

Jesus was willing to do the unconventional in the eyes of the culture in which He lived. I don't think many people at that time made the habit of separating themselves so completely from others in order to pray. And how many would have spent a whole night in prayer then, and how many would do so today? As Christians we should be willing to march to the beat of a different drum from the ordinary lifestyles of others because of the very fact we are called with a high and holy calling. I am not suggesting we should purposely try to be strange or peculiar in the eyes of others, but certainly there should be something spiritually different about us as true disciples and servants of Christ.

What if Jesus had not spent those private times in prayer as recorded in the gospels? Such a scenario should be unthinkable to us. How could Jesus ever neglect or forsake those times of communion with His heavenly Father? Prayer was His lifeline to the Father for the strength He needed to fulfill His mission successfully. Do we need any less communion with our Lord in this twenty-first century to know and fulfill God's mission for us as professed followers of Jesus Christ? Prayer is our lifeline to know the Father's will for us just as it was for Jesus (Rod Butterworth, *If My People,* Copyright © 2019 40,41).

In a general sense, why is it that in 2021 we are witnessing evil of the worst kind increasing exponentially in America on so many fronts? Even though I know there are many sincere saints of God living in this country, we would have to admit that the things we are seeing happening every day remind us of the situation in Noah's day.

"Then the Lord saw that the wickedness of man *was* great in the earth, and *that* every intent of the thoughts of his heart *was* only evil

continually...The earth was corrupt before God, and the earth was filled with violence [like America today]. **So God looked upon the earth, and indeed it was corrupt; for all flesh had corrupted their way on the earth. And God said to Noah, 'The end of all flesh has come before Me, for the earth is filled with violence through them; and behold, I will destroy them with the earth"** (Genesis 6:11-13).

Has it really become this serious in America? Unless you are oblivious to what is happening in towns and cities all across this country, you will agree that it is. So, what is the answer to the question I posed above: *Why is it that evil is increasing exponentially in America on so many fronts?* I submit that in line with the Scripture above it is because the thinking in men's hearts has become wicked and evil—**"...every intent of the thoughts of his heart *was* only evil continually."** Is there a remedy? Yes, if God's people, the true Church, will do what we are called to do as members of His body—seek God with all earnestness, with passionate intercessory prayer, and *know* by experience His power working in and through our lives on a daily basis. In other words, as individual believers who profess to be sons and daughters of God we should have Holy-Spirit-empowered ministry that the unbelieving world around us will not be able to ignore. This thought is exciting to me.

Hope for better things and a more godly society must begin with us as individuals. And if the unbelieving world observes oneness and unity in the Church by our love and compassion for one another—even if we have different opinions on the more minor matters, then we can expect more respect from unbelievers. We see that this was clearly the effect the early Church had upon their culture. It was accompanied with powerful demonstrations of the Holy Spirit's power through signs and wonders just as Jesus had promised. The record says,

"Then fear came upon every soul, and many wonders and signs were done through the apostles" (Acts 2:43); **"So great fear came upon all those who heard these things...so great fear come upon all the church and upon all who heard these things"** (Acts 5:5,11); **"And fear fell on them all, and the name of the Lord Jesus was magnified"** (Acts 19:17).

We are seeing very little, if any, of such reaction from the unbelieving world today? If so, we must not be what we are supposed to be as the Church. True, there was also severe persecution and demonic hatred of these early believers as they obeyed the Great Commission of Jesus to preach and teach the Gospel to all men. But can we not take courage from the example they have left behind of their oneness and unity of purpose? And has the modern Church by and large missed something? Have we not found the close relationship with God we need in order to experience His power as we witness for Him? Could it be that Christians today are so distracted by the schemes, temptations and secular worldly allurements of the enemy that we are not fulfilling our responsibilities as disciples of Jesus? Dare I suggest (and I speak to myself) that we may not be walking in fellowship with God as we should? Could it be that the words of the prophet Isaiah apply to us today? He wrote:

"He saw that *there was* no man, and wondered that *there was* no intercessor" (Isaiah 59:16).

There will be no effective, true intercession for revival in America until we, the Church, are living in vital intimate relationship with Him—each of us, daily in passionate and persistent prayer. How can we know the vision and heart of God unless we truly *know Him*? Until we do, we will not be seeking Him through prayer in the right way to impact our nation with a spiritual renewal that could change the hearts of men and women.

There can be no true unity among God's people until each member of the body of Christ is living in the spiritual reality of really *knowing* Him. This is something that is spiritually discerned and experienced, and although I have been a follower (imperfectly) of Jesus Christ for over sixty five years, I have found that this revelation grows to deeper levels of understanding as I continue to press on by faith. This is something that thrills and excites me as nothing else can. The potential for our lives and witness to glorify God almost seems unlimited. Paul did speak of what he found to be a tremendous thrill when he wrote of the mystery of God's blessing to the Gentiles:

"The mystery which has been hidden from ages and from generations, but now has been revealed to His saints. To them God willed to make known what are the riches of the glory of this mystery among the Gentiles; which is Christ in you, the hope of glory" (Colossians 1:26,27).

Paul is saying that by the knowledge of Christ's presence in him he has come to know increasingly **"the glory of this mystery"** which in turn brings to him the reality of **"the hope of glory."** It is by the reality of Christ's presence in him, and the fact that he knows Him intimately, that he can go about the work of the ministry with faith in the One who lives within him. He writes:

"To this *end* I also labor, striving according to His working which works in me mightily" (Colossians 1:29).

What is it that works in him mightily? Or better said: Who is it that works in him mightily as he ministers the truth? It is the active knowledge and faith in the presence of Christ within him—in his spirit/soul being. Again, this is spiritual revelation which can only come through the discipline of spending much time with Him, just as Jesus disciplined Himself to be separate from distractions in order to give His full attention to communing with the Father.

Yes, to really *know* Him is a spiritual revelation which is a marvelous yet mystical element in the life of a Christian. Judging by my own experience over the years, I know I have lived through many periods of my life when the reality of the living spiritual presence of Christ within me was a dim light of understanding to say the least. The unseen (usually) spiritual world can only be experienced when tuned into through the Holy Spirit. We can *really know Him* if we avail ourselves of the means He has provided: prayer, faith, and staying in the Word of God. Why not pause right now and experience the reality of His presence within you by faith? Thank Him and praise Him as you meditate on this wonderful truth.

Chapter 5
Finishing the Task
John 17:4

"I have glorified You on the earth. I have finished the work which You have given Me to do."

It may be encouraging to sing about heaven, but we always need to remember the reality of the fact that we have to get through this life first. Yes, Jesus truly glorified and honored His Father during His short earthly life. The Apostle Peter, who lived with Jesus and observed Him day and night for three years, gives us this testimony:

"Christ also suffered for us, leaving us an example, that you should follow His steps: *'Who committed no sin, nor was deceit found in His mouth';* who, when He was reviled, did not revile in return; when He suffered, He did not threaten, but committed *Himself* to Him who judges righteously" (1 Peter 2:21-23).

Jesus glorified the Father during His earthly ministry by staying in a close, intimate relationship with Him. By doing so He was able to know the Father's direction, will, and purpose for His daily walk on earth. In fact, Jesus did not claim to be the source of the ministry He did, which included not only His words of teaching, but also miracles of healing and deliverance from demonic influence. He did not even claim that the words He spoke were exclusively from His own mind or thinking. He said, **"The words that I speak to you I do not speak on My own *authority*; but the Father who dwells in Me does the works"** (John 14:10). Jesus was relying upon the indwelling presence of the Father to work in and through Him to produce the ministry He carried out daily. He said, **"The Father is in Me, and I in Him"** (John 10:38). Should we not take note of this, and desire the same intimate spiritual relationship for ourselves through the awesome gift and working of the Holy Spirit abiding within us? This is how the Lord can lead and guide us in our own personal ministries.

Jesus took upon Himself human flesh by submitting to a period of earthly existence for the purpose of providing redemption and salvation to a lost world. It had to be done **"on the earth"** as our scripture above says. He had to dwell with, and be identified with, the ones He came to save in order to become the perfect sacrifice for their sins. In a similar, but far less majestic way, each of us find ourselves existing *on earth* for the number of years God allows us to experience. We only have this one life and opportunity while *on earth* to be fruitful for the kingdom of God. Jesus said He had glorified the Father during His earthly sojourn, and this fact should surely challenge each of us to ask ourselves this question: Is my life and testimony on earth glorifying Jesus and the Father? If it is not, we ought to be praying earnestly that God would help us remedy the situation, because God does have a definite purpose and plan for each of us as His children.

Notice that Jesus said in His prayer He had **"finished the work which You** [the Father] **have given Me to do"** (John 17:4). There is a **"work"** which God has for each of us to do during our earthly lives. It will be a work begun, continued, and completed by faith. Let's be realistic. We will not find the ministry which God has planned for us unless we seek Him with all our hearts—prayer with fasting (see chapter 20) would be the approved biblical approach. But if we take this matter lightly with a nonchalant attitude, we will live to regret it in the future. There are so many distractions in this life which demand our attention and take our minds away from focusing on seeking God. Time is of essence. The Psalmist wrote, **"So teach *us* to number our days, that we may gain a heart of wisdom"** (Psalm 90:12).

Discernment is a gift from God that we need to help keep us on track, and if we ask God for such it will help us avoid getting involved in things unnecessary and unprofitable. This does not mean that we are so strict about our time that we cannot enjoy times of fun and fellowship with our family and friends. But keeping the eternal perspective will have the effect of lessening our desire for things of little profit. Paul writes:

"If then you were raised with Christ, seek those things which are above, where Christ is, sitting at the right hand of God. Set your mind on things above, not on things on the earth" (Colossians 3:1,2).

We have to determine not to let the influence of the world, the flesh, and the devil, keep us occupied with things that are not profitable and which keep us from finding the walk with God that produces a positive, powerful testimony through the witness of our desires, thoughts, words, and actions. This is what our lives are supposed to be before the unsaved world—positive, powerful testimonies.

A word of caution is necessary at this point. We can become so thrilled with the thought of fulfilling the Father's will for our lives and ministries, that we may eagerly grasp the first opportunity of service that comes along. There are times when I have thought I could see clearly the way ahead, only to discover later that God had a different plan. I also discovered that although I thought the original plan looked good, the real direction of God turned out to be much better. Once again, the importance of sincerely seeking the Lord for His direction is absolutely vital, or we may find ourselves entangled in an unprofitable situation that is difficult to escape from. Earnest prayer with submission of heart and mind is always the starting point.

We should remember from the first part of the key verse above that the purpose of any ministry or work is to *glorify God*. When we find and enter the ministry God has ordained for us we must remain of a humble spirit, because the only way the ministry will be successful is if it flows from His presence within us, just as we have seen demonstrated in the life of Jesus. But our enemy has many tricks up his sleeve in his attempts to derail and distract us from doing the work God has called us to do. First Peter 5:8 says:

"Be sober, be vigilant; because your adversary the devil walks about like a roaring lion, seeking whom he may devour."

We must understand the reality of the spiritual warfare we should almost certainly find ourselves encountering as Christians. I say *should,* because if we never experience any kind of spiritual attack it might be because we have not prayed prayers such as, **"Your kingdom come. Your will be done on earth as *it is* in heaven"** (Matthew 6:10). This prayer was given to us by Jesus because it is the foundation of gaining victories over Satan and his kingdom, and Satan is well aware of this. But God has provided victory for us in the daily battles we face. However, if we have not availed ourselves of the protection provided for us by Jesus we will not achieve advancement for the kingdom of God. If we allow him, Satan will cause us to waste hour after hour, week after week, and even year after year in fruitless living as far as eternal things are concerned.

This is why we have been called to know and serve the Lord. It is to further the kingdom of God on Earth until the time comes when Jesus will return and rule with righteousness. Therefore, each of us has a responsibility to fulfill the particular calling with which God has called us, and He wants each of us to be able to **"finish the work"** He has called us to do.

As we take a closer look at our lives to see if they are producing the fruit they should, we may be shocked to realize how we may have been deceived into thinking that all is well in our relationship with the Lord. One of the tricks of the enemy is what I call the *comparison game,* which is so easy for us to fall into. The Apostle Paul writes:

"For we dare not class ourselves or compare ourselves with those who commend themselves. But they, measuring themselves by themselves, and comparing themselves among themselves, are not wise" (2 Corinthians 10:12).

We must come to the understanding and realization that we are unique, individual, and each of us a one-of-a-kind special creation of God. It is obvious when looking at the marvels of creation that God loves variety. For example, it seems that all of the millions of creatures God has created in the oceans have particular niches and purposes for their existence. But an ocean creature does not have the conscious mind to wish it was something other than what it is. And this points to the difference between humans and all animals. We are the only living ones who can enjoy a special planned and guided relationship with God on an individual basis. Creatures of the ocean cannot experience this, and neither do they have consciousness of right and wrong. We are created for a much higher domain of existence than animals. The Trinitarian conversation we are privileged to have cognizance of in Scripture reads:

"Then God said, 'Let Us make man in Our image, according to Our likeness; let them have dominion over the fish of the sea, over the birds of the air, and over the cattle, over all the earth and over every creeping thing that creeps on the earth' " (Genesis 1:26).

Also:

"What is man that You are mindful of him, or the son of man that You take care of him? You have made him a little lower than the angels; You

have crowned him with glory and honor" (Hebrews 2:6,7).

We are all individually special and unique to God. Each of us has an eternal spirit/soul created by God for the purpose of being in relationship with Him. We should not be envious of others who may seem to have a better relationship with God than ourselves. The relationship God wants to have with us will be uniquely special, and we should find it, experience it, and rejoice in it. If this is a reality in our daily lives we will be at peace with ourselves and not fret or be envious of others. Our concentration should be upon developing the relationship we have ourselves as believers, and upon exercising the faith God has given us to see His purposes fulfilled through our lives.

It is the active exercising of faith in all of this that will propel us and keep us on the path of fruitful work and service for the Lord. Our desire should surely be to please our Lord in every way that we can. In the gospels, it was always the exercising of simple child-like faith that got the attention and commendation of Jesus. Hebrews 11:6 says:

"But without faith *it is* impossible to please *Him,* for he who comes to God must believe that He is, and *that* He is a rewarder of those who diligently seek Him."

Our lives should bring glory to God. In other words, we should be such examples in real life of the presence and power of Jesus to give us victory, that the attention of those who observe our lives would be directed to the One who lives within us rather than to ourselves. The Apostle Paul prayed for the Hebrew Christians that they would be mature:

"Complete in every good work to do His will, working in you what is well pleasing in His sight, through Jesus Christ, to whom *be* glory forever and ever" (Hebrews 13:21).

Yes, we can finish the work God has called us to do. Let nothing of the world, the flesh and the devil deter us from yielding ourselves to be His profitable servants. And let us rejoice daily in the privilege.

Chapter 6
Receiving and Keeping the Word
John 17:7,8

"Now they have known that all things which You have given Me are from You. For I have given to them the words which You have given Me; and they have received *them,* and have known surely that I came forth from You; and they have believed that You sent Me."

The living Word, Jesus, gave His disciples the spoken living Word which He in turn received from the Father. What an amazing privilege it was for these first disciples to be the recipients of living words directly from the Father through Jesus. These living words which we now have in our modern printed Bibles on paper with ink are given to us as they were to the disciples for the purpose of teaching and leading us into the knowledge of the truth. Not only by teaching us intellectually, but by penetrating into the inner spirit and soul of our beings. It is, of course, absolutely vital that as Christians, we *truly believe* that these words have come to us from the living God who created all things through Jesus. If we do, the Holy Spirit will make the written Word alive and active to us for application in our daily lives. The Bible is truly God's love letter and guide for carrying us through this life into the next.

Another way of looking at this is that Jesus wanted His disciples to realize that through Him they had a real and continuing connection with the Father. He had previously taught them to understand the reality of this intimate connection when He gave them guidance and instruction for prayer with the opening words, **"Our Father"** (Matthew 6:9). All true Christians are obviously praying to the same Heavenly

Father. One would think that this truth should surely foster unity and oneness among believers. But it would seem that different denominational beliefs cause many to pray to a "father" who has to adjust to a variety of theological expressions. For example, some professing Christians say that when Muslims pray to Allah it is prayer to the same God of the Bible. But the Bible, the true revelation of God's truth, says:

"For this reason I bow my knees to the Father of our Lord Jesus Christ, from whom the whole family in heaven and earth is named" (Ephesians 3:14,15).

Note from these words from Paul that it is only, **"...the Father of our Lord Jesus Christ,"** who is the true distinctive heavenly Father and divine head of all those who belong to Him, both **"...in heaven and earth."** Therefore, those who profess Christianity should realize the divine exclusive nature of the Father from all other groups who claim to have a relationship with the Creator of the universe. Any religious-minded group that discounts Jesus as God revealed in the flesh will not be able to have a close intimate relationship with the Father.

Jesus said that His disciples had openly **"received"** His words. It sounds simple enough, but as we know, men have succeeded in complicating even the words of Jesus to the extent that division is rife in the professing Church. One of the main reasons for this is the fact that people listen to certain teachers who apparently have not studied carefully enough to take the *whole Bible* into consideration when they teach. The Apostle Paul declared, **"For I have not shunned to declare to you the whole counsel of God"** (Acts 20:27).

We have a saying at our Creation Experience Museum in Branson, Missouri, when some come up with various ideas that the Bible does not clearly teach. We suggest this radical thought: *Why not accept the Bible just the way that God has given it to us?* If we could only strive with God's help to approach God's Word with this openness of mind, and to let the Word of God be the authority it is and should always be, it would surely help to foster agreement among believers. The Bible is what it is, and will always be what it is. It is not to be changed. Not added to or dissected in any way as to be lessened from what it is. In the Book of Acts there is an encouraging account of the effect evangelism had on the people in the town of Berea. Luke wrote:

"These were more fair-minded than those in Thessalonica, in that they received the word with all readiness, and searched the Scriptures daily to find out whether these things were so" (Acts 17:11).

It is evident that many are not **"fair-minded"** with the Scriptures today. This can happen after being taught supposed scriptural truth by a teacher they may respect and admire on the human level. Perhaps a personal friendship and respect between individuals may cause unconscious compromise with the **"whole counsel of God."** Just like the people of Berea, each of us, individually, should approach the meaning of Scripture with earnest prayer and a willingness to submit to its teaching with the aid of the Holy Spirit. At this point, I do not want you, the reader, to think that I am putting myself up as a supreme teacher of the Word of God. Far from it! Even after over sixty years of Bible reading and study I am still learning, and seek to humble myself with a teachable spirit every time I gaze upon those wonderfully inspired words given to us by God.

Once the disciples had willingly received the words Jesus gave them, it was their responsibility to keep them—each one individually. At the time Jesus spoke to them, I feel sure they were not aware of all that would transpire in the future as they committed themselves to live by the truths they now knew and believed. God was not going to force them to serve Him.

They were all individually responsible to answer and live by the call to ministry they had received. Judas is a sad story. Paul wrote:

"I, therefore, the prisoner of the Lord, beseech you to walk worthy of the calling with which you were called" (Ephesians 4:1). And, **Therefore do not be ashamed of the testimony of our Lord, nor of me His prisoner, but share with me in the sufferings for the gospel according to the power of God, who has saved us and called us with a holy calling, not according to our works, but according to His own purpose and grace which was given to us in Christ Jesus before time began"** (2 Timothy 1:8,9).

Yes, we have been called with a **"holy calling,"** and should seriously consider its implications with utmost humility, reverence, and respect. This spiritual *calling* is a privilege beyond description. To think and realize that in reality we are working in tandem and unity of purpose with the Creator of the universe in close intimate fellowship, is a thought which is far loftier than most others coming to mind. We should remember that such unity of spiritual cooperation is for **"His own purpose."** Our individual participation is to act the part we are called to be in harmony and teamwork with all the saints of the body of Christ. In other words, to be **"doers of the word, and not hearers only, deceiving yourselves"** (James 1:22). If all of us *do this* we will be a powerful spiritual force for the carrying out of God's plan in this present age.

In His John 17 prayer Jesus confirmed that His disciples **"have known surely that I came forth from You; and they have believed that You sent Me."** This is an amazing statement when we think below the surface meaning. Surely all professed Christians would claim to believe that Jesus came from God the Father and was sent to this earth by the Father. But for these disciples to believe Jesus was *not* born from the normal heterosexual physical union of an earthly man and woman, is absolutely staggering. Yet, if they were to be true followers of Jesus they *must* believe and accept as a historical empirical reality the virgin birth.

Not surprisingly, and sadly, in our topsy-turvy twenty-first-century world of contradictory worldviews and beliefs, there are some professed Christians who deny the virgin birth of Christ. Anyone who has fallen prey to such heretical teaching is *not* a true disciple of Jesus Christ. In fact, they would be making the same mistake that over and over again is still made today, and is the cause of divisions among Christians—departure from the absolute authority of the Word of God as our infallible guide for faith and practice. It is significant that Luke was inspired to be very specific and clear about Christ's virgin birth when he wrote the words **"(as was supposed)."**

"Now Jesus Himself began *His ministry at* about thirty years of age, being (as was supposed) *the* son of Joseph, *the son* of Heli" (Luke 3:23).

Also, Matthew, being one of the original disciples who had been present with Jesus during His earthly ministry, made it very clear that he had no doubt about the virgin birth of Jesus when he recorded the words of Isaiah 7:14:

"Behold, the virgin shall be with child, and bear a Son, and they shall call His name Immanuel," which is translated, 'God with us' "** (Matthew 1:23).

Not only was it necessary for the disciples to believe Jesus came from the Father, but they also needed to believe the Father had sent Jesus for a divine, specific purpose. This is part and parcel of the Gospel which the disciples would be intimately involved with for the rest of their lives. They were to be the first to boldly spread the message that Jesus was truly the

Messiah sent into the world to bring salvation to all who would believe. This is why the truth of the virgin birth is so crucial. How could people believe Jesus was anything other than totally ordinary if His appearance in this world as a child was through the same physical means of sexual reproduction as humankind in general? Also, belief in Jesus' resurrection is likewise equally just as crucial to Christianity. In fact, even beyond acceptance of the virgin birth, belief and full acceptance of the resurrection of Christ is absolutely essential to the foundation of Christianity.

We should surely be awestruck, even mystified, by the knowledge that Jesus, the eternal Son of God, was willing to subject Himself to physical life on the planet He Himself created. Especially so since He knew in advance the details of the agonizing suffering He would endure on a cruel Roman cross. Not just the physical suffering, but the spiritual suffering by carrying the weight and sins of all people. Jesus, the second but coequal member of the Godhead, was willing to come even though it meant temporary separation from the Father. In John's Gospel we notice the importance of the truth that Jesus was *sent* by the emphasis the Holy Spirit gives to it numerous times. Let the truth sink into your heart as you prayerfully read these words of Jesus (notice the word *sent* throughout):

"For He whom God has sent speaks the words of God, for God does not give the Spirit by measure" (John 3:34).

"Jesus said to them, 'My food is to do the will of Him who sent Me, and to finish His work' " (John 4:34).

"He who does not honor the Son does not honor the Father who sent Him" (John 5:23).

"Most assuredly, I say to you, he who hears My word and believes in Him who sent Me has

everlasting life, and shall not come into judgment, but has passed from death into life" (John 5:24).

"I do not seek My own will but the will of the Father who sent Me" (John 5:30).

"For the works which the Father has given Me to finish—the very works that I do—bear witness of Me, that the Father has sent Me" (John 5:36).

"And the Father Himself, who sent Me, has testified of Me. You have neither heard His voice at any time, nor seen His form" (John 5:37).

"But you do not have His word abiding in you, because whom He sent, Him you do not believe" (John 5:38).

"Jesus answered and said to them, 'This is the work of God, that you believe in Him whom He sent' " (John 6:29).

"For I have come down from heaven, not to do My own will, but the will of Him who sent Me" (John 6:38).

"This is the will of the Father who sent Me, that of all He has given Me I should lose nothing, but should raise it up at the last day" (John 6:39).

"And this is the will of Him who sent Me, that everyone who sees the Son and believes in Him may have everlasting life; and I will raise him up at the last day" (John 6:40).

"No one can come to Me unless the Father who sent Me draws him; and I will raise him up at the last day" (John 6:44).

"As the living Father sent Me, and I live because of the Father, so he who feeds on Me will live because of Me" (John 6:57).

"Jesus answered them and said, 'My doctrine is not Mine, but His who sent Me' " (John 7:16).

"He who speaks from himself seeks his own glory; but He who seeks the glory of the One who

sent Him is true, and no unrighteousness is in Him" (John 7:18).

What would be our best response to the truths of these words of Jesus? I believe it would be to yield to the divine commission all of us have received from Jesus when, after His glorious resurrection, He said to His disciples and by extension to all of us, **"As the Father has sent Me, I also send you"** (John 20:21).

The Father sent Jesus for the all-encompassing purpose of redeeming a lost world that had lost its way since the Garden of Eden. What is our calling today? It is to be sent just as Jesus was sent by the Father. The question is: Are we willing to be sent? Are we willing to receive and keep the Word by being obedient to the commission we have received from our Lord? If we are, we will be doing our part to see the prayer of Jesus answered when He prayed,

"I do not pray for these alone, but also for those who will believe in Me through their word; that they all may be one, as You, Father, are in Me, and I in You; that they also may be one in Us, that the world may believe that You sent Me" (John 17:20,21).

Chapter 7
Directed Prayer
John 17:9

"I pray for them. I do not pray [Greek, *eroto ou*—make request] **for the world but for those whom You have given Me, for they are Yours."**

If you are a true believer Jesus is praying for you. At this time when He was with the eleven disciples He wanted to concentrate His prayer specifically on them. Jesus knew that if He prayed for those who are His, they will be strengthened spiritually and willingly obey His command to reach the world with the Gospel. Amazingly, Jesus was committing the future of His Church to this small band of very unimpressive ordinary people. When He appeared to them in Galilee after His resurrection He said:

"Go therefore and make disciples of all the nations, baptizing them in the name of the Father and of the Son and of the Holy Spirit, teaching them to observe all things that I have commanded you; and lo, I am with you always, *even* to the end of the age" (Matthew 28:19,20).

As Jesus continues to pray for His Church today He passionately desires that the work and impact of the Gospel will be effectively accomplished. Preeminently, for the unsaved to be reached, and that many will begin their journey of salvation. This is why He was willing to give His life on the cross. But just because it is Jesus doing the praying, and surely His prayers are the most powerful of all prayers, is this a guarantee that the whole world will be reached automatically? No, it takes the willing cooperation and obedience of the people of God working in harmony with the Holy Spirit. The principle we see in the Scriptures is that God is always ready to do His part if we will do ours. Faith is a vital part of our successful relationship with Him, because we will only be His willing servants to serve Him faithfully if we have faith in His faithfulness. This is not to be confused with salvation by human effort or works. Jesus said, **"This is the *work* of God, that you *believe* in Him whom He sent"** (John 6:29, emphasis mine).

The Scriptures indicate that Jesus not only prays for the Church corporately, but for each of us as individual believers. What awesome and glorious knowledge this should be to all of us! Are we really absorbing this incredible truth that our Creator prays for us? It should fill our hearts with faith and expectant joy as we meditate on this truth of His concern for us individually. The realization of this fact should also humble us with an overwhelming sense of reverential awe that it is the Creator of the universe who is praying for us—or we could even say individually, *for me.*

Jesus directs prayer for His children very specifically. Peter, the beloved apostle who seemed to say the wrong things more than once (haven't we all?), was the recipient of Jesus' prayer when he most likely did not think he needed it. He was not aware of the fact that Satan had **"asked"** for him—obviously with evil intentions. Jesus said to him:

"Simon, Simon! Indeed, Satan has asked for you, that he may sift you as wheat. But I have prayed for you, that your faith should not fail; and when you have returned to Me, strengthen your brethren" (Luke 22:31).

As we experience a closer relationship with the Lord, we will get more insight into our individual needs as well as those of others, and then we will be encouraged to know that Jesus is praying the perfect prayer for us. After all, He knows everything about us. He knew exactly how to pray for Peter because He knew his heart and what he would need to be victorious in his personal life and witness for the Lord. There is nothing hidden from Him. So, just like Jesus, we should learn to be very specific in our prayers as we sense the leading and direction of the Holy Spirit. I doubt that prayers which are too general will reap many beneficial results, so we should seek the Lord until we sense the voice of the Lord bringing to our minds the petitions for which we should be seeking Him in prayer. Jesus said,

"Therefore I say to you, whatever things you ask when you pray, believer that you receive *them*, and you will have *them*" (Mark 11:24).

Therefore, with all this in mind we should realize how vital it is to have such a close relationship with the Lord to clearly hear His voice and know how we should pray. We should seek the Lord to receive His leading on how to pray for this matter so close to His heart— spiritual oneness and unity of true Christians in the body of Christ. This is obviously of huge concern to Jesus as we see Him passionately praying this prayer in John 17. If oneness among believers was and is of such great concern to Jesus, it obviously should be of great concern to us today. We need to understand spiritually that by praying in earnest for unity in the body of Christ, we are also uniting with Jesus in prayer for the reaching of lost souls with the Gospel.

It is only when the people of God are alive with the same vibrant passion for unity and the spreading of the good news of the Gospel, that anything of lasting eternal value can be accomplished for the kingdom of God. But we can note from the past experience of the Church that God chooses to start with the individual. It is individual revival and intimate relationship with the Lord which sets the stage for the Holy Spirit to impact those around us with His divine holy presence. As we position ourselves with faith, humility, and submission before the Lord, He will delight to answer our prayers by His Spirit working in and through us.

Let us remember from the words of Jesus that we belong to the Father. Jesus referred to us when He prayed to the Father with the words, **"they are Yours."** Do we sense the nearness of the Father as we seek our Triune God in prayer? Have we thought of the Father as rather beyond our reach spiritually as far as fellowship with Him is concerned? If so, we have missed great blessing. Does not John 3:16 remind us that **"God so loved"** that He, the Father, sent Jesus to be the sacrifice for our sins on the cross? Here is the truth: God the Father loves us; Jesus loves us; and the Holy Spirit loves us. Have we really grasped this incredible truth for ourselves individually? Our Triune God is an extremely personal God!

What is the present situation in America today as a nation historically known as Christian? We are in desperate need of a nation-wide spiritual awakening and renewal to bring our people back to God-consciousness and biblical values of morality. Such could only begin to come to pass as a reality when accompanied with a powerful awareness of God through the convicting work of the Holy Spirit. It was said of the revival that began in 1949 in the Hebrides islands off of Scotland, that there was a powerful *awareness of God* that seemed to permeate the whole community. In America in the 2020s, we desperately need our church leaders to boldly declare the need for spiritual renewal and restoration, political integrity, and a return to biblical moral standards in order to repair the damage done to our nation in previous years.

However, these church leaders must be full of the power of the Holy Spirit through humbling themselves to seek God, or little will be accomplished. Just as Paul prayed for the believers in the incipient churches he ministered to in the first century, so we today must pick up the challenge and pray for one another earnestly. Have we lacked praying for our true brothers and sisters in Christ because of different denominational name tags? To my shame I must confess guilt of this charge myself. Here is a passionate prayer from the heart of the Apostle Paul which should challenge all of us. He wrote:

"For this reason I bow my knees to the Father of our Lord Jesus Christ, from whom the whole family in heaven and earth is named, that He would grant you, according to the riches of His glory, to be strengthened with might through His Spirit in the inner man, that Christ may dwell in your hearts through faith; that you, being rooted and grounded in love, may be able to comprehend with *all the saints* what is the width and length and depth and height—to know the love of Christ which passes knowledge; that you may be filled with all the fullness of God" (Ephesians 3:14-19, emphasis mine).

What is the central desire of this prayer Paul prayed for the Christians in the Church at Ephesus? It has to do with the spiritual condition of the **"inner man."** God is always concerned with the *inner* first because the *outer* will naturally spring forth from the *inner*. In other words, as it says, Christ must dwell in our hearts through faith so that the love of God can flow unhindered from our innermost beings to those around us. Although Paul is praying for the Church as a whole, it comes down to the individual to personally respond for anything of lasting eternal value to result. We have individual responsibility. It is not us, but Who is working in and through us that becomes real spiritual ministry. Therefore, Paul prays for the Ephesian Christians to be **"filled with all the fullness of God."**

Just stop for a moment and consider the meaning of these words, to think that you and I, as Christians, can be and should be **"filled with all the fullness of God."** It reminds me of the words of David in Psalm 23:5 when he wrote, **"You anoint my head with oil, my cup runs over."** Yet we will often find our lives filled with many other things, interests, occupations and activities that do not give evidence of an overflowing life of God's presence.

What a wonderful example Paul's prayer is for us to emulate as we pray for revival and unity of the body of Christ in America and around the world. This love Paul talks about **"passes knowledge"** which means it surpasses and exceeds any degree of love found in natural relationships. Even though this amazing level of love is beyond generating from within our natural selves, Paul says we can **"know the love of Christ"** in a very personal and individual way.

Jesus wanted His disciples to have an intimate loving relationship with the Father in real-life everyday experience. Here is a very significant fact indicated by the life of Jesus: *He valued His personal relationship with the Father during His earthly ministry above all other relationships and everything else.* This last sentence should immediately cause us to have thoughts of self-examination. How much do we show by our lives the value of our personal relationship with the Father through Jesus? The disciples Jesus had chosen and was praying for had been with Him for three years, but there was still a lot of spiritual growth needed. Jesus knew the challenging future they would soon be facing. He wanted them to truly believe in the words of His assurance to them that He would always be with them. Also, the Heavenly Father would always be there as a Father to them through the ministry of the Holy Spirit. This is truth that all Christians should be aware of and encourage one another with as they travel through all of life's experiences. Children eventually lose their earthly father, but what a comfort to know the love of our Heavenly Father whom we can always approach through Jesus Christ.

This prayer of Jesus is an example given for us to emulate. We should take very seriously our responsibility to pray for one another in the body of

Christ. Read the strong language written by the Apostle Paul to exhort the believers in Rome to pray for him:

"Now I beg you, brethren, through the Lord Jesus Christ, and through the love of the Spirit, that you strive together with me in prayers to God for me, that I may be delivered from those in Judea who do not believe, and that my service for Jerusalem may be acceptable to the saints" (Romans 15:30,31).

He says they should **"strive together"** with him in prayer. How do we spend the hours of our days? Do we think of praying even once or twice a day? Is there a real sense of the Holy Spirit's presence with us moment by moment as we go about our daily activities? Do we offer thanksgiving on a regular basis for God's overriding protection as we travel on dangerous roads and airways? Have we carelessly told someone we would pray for them but fail to do it? I know such questions as these will bring conviction and regret for those with sensitive hearts to the Spirit of God. Most of us would have to be honest enough to admit that we have not prayed as we ought.

Paul prays in the scripture above that it is **"through the love of the Spirit"** we should pray for one another. There are times when we need prayer to be **"delivered"** from some who may hinder our witness for Christ and the Gospel. If we have the same compassionate heart and love for our brothers and sisters that Jesus has, we will find ourselves compelled to offer intercession for those facing difficult situations. Jesus reminds us of the importance of the second greatest commandment which is: **"You shall love your neighbor as yourself"** (Matthew 22:39). As we naturally look after ourselves, we should have the same concern for other members of the body of Christ.

The Apostle Paul effectively uses the human body to illustrate the truth of spiritual unity among Christians. He wrote:

"For as the body is one and has many members, but all the members of that one body, being many, are one body, so also *is* Christ. For by one Spirit we were all baptized into one body—whether Jews or Greeks, whether slaves or free—and have all been made to drink into one Spirit" (1 Corinthians 12:12,13).

First, Paul says, we should recognize our spiritual oneness by reason of the fact that we have come into relationship with God by the same means—being born again through the regenerating ministry of the Holy Spirit. Then Paul continues:

"For in fact the body is not one member but many. If the foot should say, 'Because I am not a hand, I am not of the body,' is it therefore not of the body? And if the ear should say, 'Because I am not an eye, I am not of the body,' Is it therefore not of the body?" (1 Corinthians 12:14-16).

Anyone who loses the function of a physical body part knows how valuable that missing part is. Something as basic to most people as the ability to walk becomes unbelievably precious to those who for various reasons lose that which was formerly taken for granted. Paul continues:

"If the whole body *were* an eye, where *would be* the hearing? If the whole *were* hearing, where *would be* the smelling? But God has set the members, each one of them, in the body just as He pleased. If they *were* all one member, where *would* the body be?" (1 Corinthians 12:17-19).

Paul wants to make absolutely sure that his readers get the message by expanding this illustration of the human body. The main point he wants to get across is that we *belong* to Christ and the Father, and what we experience in life should be of great interest and concern to all the members of the spiritual body of the Church. Paul concludes the illustration with these defining words, **"Now you are the body of Christ, and members individually"** (1 Corinthians 12:27).

Yes, the wonderful truth of belonging to the Lord as God's people is most powerfully realized by personal individual experience. But how meaningful and deep our sense of belonging is to the Lord depends on whether we fully enter into the relationship available to us through individual personal intimacy with Him. If we are serious about this the Lord will minister to us through His Spirit, who will then guide us in our individual callings for ministry. Can we joyfully say with holy abandonment: I am His, and He is mine?

Chapter 8
Reflected glory
John 17:10

"And all Mine are Yours, and Yours are Mine, and I am glorified in them."

Ownership! Belonging to someone else can be a positive or negative thing. I could say that I belong to my wife and she belongs to me, and this is a good thing because God has put us together as man and wife in a loving and committed relationship.

After graduating from high school in England, I began a five-year apprenticeship with a printing company. I became legally bound to serve that company until those years were completed. In other words, I literally belonged to them as an employee for that period of time and could not leave to work for another company. But at the same time, the company was legally obligated to keep me as an employee for five years even if I turned out to be a failure for some reason. In some parts of the world today slavery still exists in various forms and would almost always be considered a bad thing. But the Apostle Paul counted it a privilege to refer to himself as, **"Paul, a bondservant of Jesus Christ"** (Romans 1:1). So, it all depends on what kind of relationship we are talking about that exists between an owner and the one or ones owned.

Clearly, Jesus is talking about extremely close personal relationships like those between Himself, the Father, the Holy Spirit and true believers. Again, using the marriage relationship as an illustration, we understand that to be in a situation such as Jesus is talking about, there would need to be a harmonious blending and sharing of intimate, transparent, and surrendered personalities to the will of God. There would need to be a relinquishing of what we could consider to be one's personal rights and independent existence accompanied by an unreserved willingness to be molded and shaped in agreement with the will of another. This relationship would be reciprocal. The prayer of Jesus in the Garden of Gethsemane is a perfect example of this:

"O My Father, if it is possible, let this cup pass from Me; nevertheless, not as I will, but as You *will*" (Matthew 26:39).

Three times Jesus prayed this prayer of complete surrender to the Father's will. He wanted to make sure that the circumstance in which He found Himself proceeded in perfect harmony with the leading, direction, and intention of His Father. Now, to apply this to the subject at hand we can see that for the body of Christ to be truly one in unity, we must have the same commitment to be and do whatever is best for the glory of God—not necessarily related to our own personal ministry. At this point we could individually ask ourselves on a personal level: Am I yielded to the Lord's will for my life to the extent I have placed myself unreservedly into His hands for His purposes to be fulfilled, rather than my own? And, am I willing to be an active part in the team of the body of Christ rather than an independent-minded maverick who always tries to do things *my way*? Do I mean what I say when I make the commitment to serve *the Lord*?

Matthew recorded the time Jesus talked about two sons and their relationship with their father:

"A man had two sons, and he came to the first and said, 'Son, go, work today in my vineyard.' He answered and said, 'I will not,' but afterward he regretted it and went. Then he came to the second and said likewise. And he answered and said, 'I go sir,' but he did not go. Which of the two did the will of *his* father? They said to Him, 'The first.' Jesus said to them, 'Assuredly, I say to

you that tax collectors and harlots enter the kingdom of God before you' " (Matthew 21:28-31).

If we really mean what we say from our hearts we will reveal which of these two sons we identify with. We could say that both of them *belonged* to the father, but only one was honest enough to admit his mistake and make the necessary correction to obey. One of the most difficult things for Christians to remember through the experiences and challenges of each day is that we are not called to make decisions based on our emotional feelings of the moment. We should ask the Holy Spirit to help us live with the consciousness of His presence within us. As we develop this with the help of the Lord we will be able to respond to our daily environment and the people we encounter with love, the wisdom of God and the fruit of the Spirit.

If we claim Jesus as our Lord and Savior, we should have the truth engraved into our consciousness that **"all Mine are yours."** In other words, if we belong to Jesus we also belong to the Father. It is God, through Jesus, who has made it possible for us to be lifted up by His strength and set free from our sinful acts and tendencies. It is only with His help we can even begin to become like Jesus and live a victorious life. Personally, it comes down to each of us being willing to confess: "I am not my own."

Jesus ended His account of the two sons with a powerful reminder of the consequences of our choices while living our short lives on this earth. He said to the religious leaders: **"Assuredly, I say to you that tax collectors and harlots enter the kingdom of God before you."** Meaning by this, that self-righteousness will lead to a possible lost eternity, whereas those who humbly repent of their sinfulness and ask for forgiveness of their sins will experience entrance into the future glories of Heaven.

Jesus said of those who believe in Him, **"I am glorified in them"** (John 17:10). A basic question we should be willing to face is: Do our lives bring glory to God? This would lead us to think about how our lives appear outwardly to those around us by the way we conduct ourselves. But I believe *who we are* in the inner core of our beings is far more important and significant than *what we do.* Because even though we may appear to be doing the correct things outwardly to glorify God, if our inner spiritual state and relationship with the Lord is not as it should be, then what we do will not have the spiritual impact and influence upon others that it otherwise could. In other words, people should become aware of something different about the quality of our lives as Christians, not so much because of what we are doing, but because there is a spiritual influence in the very atmosphere around us. When people spend time with us they should sense a spiritual presence that causes them to think about their spiritual state rather than about us as individuals. This will only happen as we are filled with the Holy Spirit on a daily basis.

The conversation Jesus had with the Samaritan woman in John chapter four is an example of how the presence of Jesus can impact people who are least expecting any such experience. The woman was going about her daily chores when to her surprise she found herself interacting with someone who somehow knew how to reach into her secret innermost being with startling accuracy. This was also an encounter that naturally should not have had any positive outcome. The reason for this being that, for a long time, there lacked any acceptance or harmonious relationships between the Jews and Samaritans. In fact, there was strong avoidance, distrust and disdain, even hatred between these two theologically opposed groups, which is why the woman said in surprise, **"How is it that You, being a Jew, ask a drink from me, a Samaritan woman?"** (v. 9). John then makes it clear that the division between Jews and Samaritans was one that was generally known and accepted by adding, **"For Jews have no dealings with Samaritans"** (v. 9).

Can we see an application from this account to the divisions we know exist among professed Christians today? This is obvious when we admit that Christians have for hundreds of years (including America in colonial days) used theologically based denominational names to identify themselves as distinct from one another. Do we really think God experiences pleasure to observe His people separating themselves in worship and fellowship as Presbyterians, Southern Baptists, Freewill Baptists, Reformed, Lutherans, Methodists, Anglicans, Pentecostals, Church of Christ, Episcopalians, Nazarenes, so-called nondenominational, and many other varieties of distinctions? The answer should be obvious, but any viable solution would seem well beyond the reach and understanding of even the most intelligent and spiritually wise among us. Yet, we know God cannot be happy with the current situation. However, the words of Jesus to the woman at the well do tell us what God is really looking for in His true followers. He said:

"Woman, believe Me, the hour is coming when you will neither on this mountain, nor in Jerusalem, worship the Father. You worship what you do not know; we know what we worship, for salvation is of the Jews. But the hour is coming, and now is, when the true worshipers will worship the Father in spirit and truth; for the Father is seeking such to worship Him. God is Spirit, and those who worship Him must worship in spirit and truth" (John 4:21-24).

In other words, Jesus was concerned about teaching the true approach to worshiping God. The emphasis of both Jews and Samaritans was on the visible outward ceremonial and geographical locations (buildings) in which they carried out their worship. But Jesus wanted to get across to this woman what was really the most important. It is the attitude of the individual heart that is most crucial as far as God is concerned. He is looking for **"true worshipers."** The words **"in spirit and truth"** emphasize again that it is the inner expression of worship based on divine truth which is acceptable to God. The problem is that theologically, we argue over what *truth* is just like the Jews and Samaritans. Because of this, we could say that protestant evangelical churches today are not bringing glory to Jesus as they should and could because they are projecting obvious disunity to the world at large.

The problem of this visible disunity amongst us as brothers and sisters in Christ seems unsolvable from a human point of view. Organizationally, it would seem we are stuck with where we currently are as institutions perpetuating division, even if the sentiment and desire exist for unity to be expressed for the world to see that we are really one at heart and in spirit. Bible scholar Donald Stamps writes:

> "Attempting to create what looks like unity by having meetings, conferences or complex organization can result in tension and frustration. What Jesus had in mind is much more than unified gatherings or the appearance of togetherness. It is a spiritual unity of heart, mind and purpose among those who are fully devoted to Christ and His Word . . . This does not mean that God's people must agree or have the same perspective on all issues, but they must maintain a unified and uncompromising commitment to honoring Christ, staying true to his Word and leading others into a personal relationship with God" (Donald C. Stamps. *Fire Bible*. Springfield MO: Life Publishers Inter-national, Study Notes, 2014 1506).

Attempts have been, and are being made by various church leaders to show the watching world a united Church. However, this is mainly by ecumenical councils with involvement in social and altruistic concerns to meet the physical and environmental needs of the poor and underprivileged. These efforts can seem worthy of praise at first, but then one finds that because of the sensitivity to avoid upsetting any participating groups theologically, the crucial message of the Gospel and salvation as exclusively attained through Jesus Christ alone is diluted to meaninglessness. Leslie Woodson writes:

"If Jesus is the world's only Savior we dare not divert our mission into channels of service emptied of the opportunity or responsibility of announcing Christ as the one and only solution for man's plight. Improving the social and economic situations of the needy are important parts of any valid missionary work. It has always been so. But the earlier version of missions as winning men to the Christ must be central [referring to the early Church's ministry as seen in the Book of Acts]. And it must not be hidden under the cloak of humanitarian labor as though the non-Christian will discover this secret in our compassion. The name of Jesus must be on our lips always and the claim of Christ upon the whole world must be the eternal imperative in our work." (Leslie Woodson. *The Church United or Untied?* The Zondervan Corporation, Grand Rapids. Copyright, 1974 39).

So, Woodson is saying we must always share the Gospel verbally and boldly just as the early disciples did from the Day of Pentecost in the first century. Did the lives and witness of the first disciples glorify Jesus? Absolutely. And they glorified Jesus while facing severe persecution by their expressed unity and oneness of purpose. We see an amazing unity among the first early believers, which resulted in souls responding to the Gospel. Luke recorded:

"Now all who believed were together, and had all things in common, and sold their possessions and goods, and divided them among all, as anyone had need. So continuing daily with one accord in the temple, and breaking bread from house to house, they ate their food with gladness and simplicity of heart, praising God and having favor with all the people. And the Lord added to the church daily those who were being saved"** (Acts 2:44-47).

Yes, one can clearly see the effectiveness of the Church when unity of purpose binds Christians together in obeying the words of Jesus to **"be witnesses to Me in Jerusalem, and in all Judea and Samaria, and to the end of the earth"** (Acts 1:8). When Christians are engaged in total commitment to the work of the Gospel, they will be less likely to bring up petty details which would produce disunity. It should be remembered as a basic principle and reality that lack of unity among believers will not bring glory to Jesus.

The above scripture in Acts does let us know that concern for physical and material needs was included as part of their unity in serving the Lord. But when we read, **"And the Lord added to the church daily those who were being saved,"** it is obvious that the most important activity these early disciples were engaged in was obeying the words of Jesus to be witnesses for the Gospel. Their main concern was for lost people to be saved by repenting of their sins and believing in Jesus as their Messiah and Savior.

By obeying the will of God as revealed to them through Jesus the early disciples impacted their culture powerfully. Being full of the Holy Spirit they glorified Jesus by reflecting His glory through their words and actions. But it was not just the outward expression of their faith and obedience to Jesus, it was the very powerful presence of the Holy Spirit who flowed out of their inner beings to those around them. However, we should note that miracles, signs and wonders were an integral part of their ministry—still a missing ingredient in conservative evangelical churches today in America. Because of their complete abandonment to the cause of Jesus the Holy Spirit was free to do His work of conviction through them. It was so powerful that it was recorded of Stephen the first Christian martyr as he spoke before the religious leaders: **"And all who sat in the council, looking steadfastly at him, saw his face as the face of an angel"** (Acts 6:15).

Stephen truly reflected Jesus' glory, and his dedication even to the martyr's death for the sake of the Gospel surely grabs our hearts with conviction to wonder if anything like this could ever be said about us. Whether we think of ourselves individually or corporately as the Church, we know we should be instruments revealing to the world around us the evidence of Jesus' glorious presence. If we are willing to let the Spirit deal with each one of us according to His will, I believe there will be hope for Jesus to find us doing that which is pleasing in His sight. May it be our true desire to be among those who glorify Him.

Chapter 9
Earthbound Unity
John 17:11

"Now I am no longer in the world, but these are in the world, and I come to You. Holy Father, keep through Your name those whom You have given Me, that they may be one as We *are*."

We may sometimes get to the stage in our thinking where we wish we were already beyond this physical life and were enjoying the future blessings of heaven in the presence of our Lord. But while we are still **"in the world,"** as Jesus says, we must face the fact that we have a job to do. Adam and Eve experienced a blissful environment in the Garden of Eden, but they were still required to actively **"tend and keep it"** as God's gardeners (Genesis 2:15).

Recliners can be dangerous! God never intended for us to settle down in luxurious comfort on an eternal beautiful tropical beach somewhere with attendants supplying our every need. Neither will we be sitting in heavenly ethereal clouds strumming on harps for all eternity. Although some may not like to hear it, the Bible does not speak of retirement from the Lord's work. An example comes to mind. A few days before he died in 1947, the well-known powerful evangelist Smith Wigglesworth said at the age of 87:

"Today in my mail I had an invitation to [minister in] Australia, one to India and Ceylon, and one to America." (Albert Hibbert. *Smith Wigglesworth: The Secret of his Power*. Harrison House, Tulsa, 1982 14).

A week later while at a church and planning to participate in a funeral service, Wigglesworth suddenly went to be with the Lord with no apparent illness. He appeared healthy and strong to the last. I've often told my wife that this is the way I would like to go when my time comes—with my boots on!

As Christians we are called to be about the Lord's business. We may not always feel like it, but when we are obedient by engaging in the work of God, we will soon find fulfillment and satisfaction that cannot be attained any other way. The reason why we find ourselves living in the world at this particular time in history is because God has a unique and special plan for each of us. He knows we have been created with special gifts for the purpose of fulfilling the tasks He has called us to do during our short earthly existence. Surely none of us would want to miss God's special plan that He has for us, and live with regrets for all eternity?

Since none of us had the choice of deciding what time in history we entered this physical world, we should be serious about finding God's divine purpose for our existence in our God-ordained timespan on this earth. We ought to be willing and submissive to do as the Apostle Paul challenged first-century Christians regarding their relationship with the world. We should know what to avoid and what to embrace if we truly desire to please God. Paul wrote:

"And do not be confirmed to this world, but be transformed by the renewing of your mind, that you may prove what *is* that good and acceptable and perfect will of God" (Romans 12:2).

God does have a specific will and purpose for each of His children, and if we diligently apply ourselves with faith and prayer, He will surely reveal it to us. We can be sure that whatever His purpose is for each one of us, it will be to work in harmony and unity with other servants of the Lord. Jesus was soon to leave His thirty-three-year earthly sojourn and said to the Father, **"I come to You."** What then, was His main concern for the disciples since they would be left behind to live out their allotted time on Earth? He prayed for them to be kept. He said, **"Keep through Your name those whom You have given Me."**

Question: Why did Jesus feel the need to pray that His followers would be *kept*? In what way would these disciples need to be kept, and kept from what?

This raises a theological matter that will most likely make some of certain belief systems feel uncomfortable because of what has been accepted and taught for so long. But we should always let the Bible speak for itself. After all, every word contained in it is inspired by the Holy Spirit.

Again, why did Jesus see the *need* to pray such a prayer for His disciples to be *kept*? Wasn't the salvation of His first disciples and their individual eternal destiny secure? Wasn't their relationship with Jesus something that was guaranteed to continue indefinitely? Were they not going to be sealed with the Holy Spirit? Wasn't it true that nothing could break their unity with Christ? Following is one scripture of *many* that could be mentioned to give us perspective and understanding on this question. On the Day of Pentecost after Peter's Holy-Spirit-inspired message we read:

"And the Lord added to the church daily such as should be saved" (Acts 2:47 KJV).

The Greek word for **"saved"** in this verse is *sozomenous* in the present continuous tense which means "being saved." This throws a different light on understanding what *being saved* means. As true born-again believers we are told by some that once we have been saved through a one-time prayer of true repentance, there is no alternative except to be guaranteed future residency in Heaven for eternity (after the prayer of true repentance I prefer to say the more scripturally supported explanation that we have started our spiritual journey of salvation). It is inferred that such a guarantee is true regardless of how life is lived from this time on, whether righteously or unrighteously. So why did Jesus pray the way He did? He must have thought it vitally important to do so. Here is the reason: He knows there is great spiritual danger for Christians while living their physical lives on Earth, and His prayer for them to be safely kept through such dangerous territory is therefore an extremely important and necessary prayer. There are numerous warnings given specifically to believers throughout the Bible that need to be taken very seriously. Eternal destiny is at stake.

With these thoughts in mind, we could ask whether there is an implication or inference contained in Jesus' prayer that some of His followers might *not* be safely and securely kept to enjoy future eternity after life on Earth. His prayer makes no logical sense unless we accept this as a real possibility. Jesus wants those who trust in Him to arrive safely and be with Him in that eternal heavenly realm. He desires for us to experience glorious intimate relationship with Him for all eternity. He surely also desires His people to begin experiencing wonderful spiritual unity while on Earth as a precursor to Heaven.

The best way to enter by experience into unity among professed Christians is to first of all recognize the invisible *spiritual unity* of all believers. We should clearly understand and accept the reality that all of us need the prayer of Jesus to keep us in strong relationship with Him throughout our earthly lives. So whatever particular earthly spiritual fellowship or denomination we have aligned ourselves with, it is vital we fully recognize as true brothers and sisters those who are also needy recipients of this prayer of Jesus.

In our chapter's verse Jesus prayed **"keep through Your name."** What did Jesus mean by referring to the name of the Father? Names are important. Most people are proud of their natural family names and would not want to change them. The Father's name as revealed in the Scriptures is multifaceted. For example, seven scriptural names of God include: *Jehovah Jireh*, the Lord will provide (Genesis 22:14); *Jehovah Tsidkenu*, The Lord our Righteousness (Jeremiah 23:6); *Jehovah Shalom*, The Lord is Peace (Judges 6:24); *Jehovah Raah,* The Lord is my Shepherd (Psalm 23:1); *Jehovah Rapha,* The Lord who Heals (Exodus 15:26); *Jehovah Nissi,* The Lord is my Banner (Exodus 17:15); *Jehovah Shammah, The Lord is There,* (Ezekiel 48:35).

You will notice the first name of *Jehovah Jireh* on this list. Meaning: "The Lord will provide." This characteristic of God was revealed when Abraham's faith was tested. He was asked to sacrifice Isaac, his beloved and long-awaited special son of promise. It is surely extremely difficult for most of us to relate to the amazing dedication and obedience we observe in the life of Abraham during this incident! But God had *provided* a ram for the sacrifice, Isaac was saved, and Abraham passed the test with an incredible demonstration of faith. This dramatic incident reminds us that when we are faced with a test where there seems no known way out of it, the Lord is always able to *provide* the solution.

As Jesus purposefully prayed, we certainly need to be *kept* as the faithful body of Christ during the almost unbelievable increase of sin and evil in our present world. In America we are seeing more and more overt public resistance to anything related to God, the Bible, and Christianity. Some predict severe persecution will be the experience of American Christians in the not-too-distant future. Our spiritual enemy, Satan, is surely working ceaselessly to bring down the influence of biblical Christianity to cultural meaninglessness if he can. With such in mind we should be able to understand the need for God's people to be united in spiritual strength to face the enemy fearlessly in the power and demonstration of the Holy Spirit.

God revealed Himself to Moses as the great **"I AM"** and in Exodus 3:14 we read:

"And God said to Moses, 'I AM WHO I AM.' And He said, 'Thus you shall say to the children of Israel, 'I AM has sent me to you.' "

The words, **"I am"** would indicate an eternally present and active God who is very much involved in the affairs of His creation. God is not like the god of the deist or the agnostic who supposedly started creation of the universe but then left it to its own devices, and who may not even exist. No, the God of the Bible is the One and only ever-present God who actually desires an individual, personal, and intimate relationship with His creation. Since this is what we learn from the Bible about God and His desire for relationship with us, we should also realize that He desires the members of His spiritual body to likewise relate to one another with love and unity.

Jesus said, **"keep through Your name those whom You have given Me, that they may be one as We** *are.*" Straight forward exegesis (grammatical historical interpretation) would mean that Jesus is saying His disciples and followers would not **"be one"** unless they are being kept in a continuing relationship with their Lord. It starts with individuals. That is, each of us as professed followers of Jesus Christ is required to respond by faith to God's invitation to be in an intimate relationship with Him. If we as individuals are not where we should be in our relationship with the Lord, we cannot expect to see real spiritual unity demonstrated in the body of Christ as a whole. Leslie Woodson writes:

> "Jesus Christ is the son of God who died for our sins, rose from the dead, and will come again. That is the core of our faith as Christians. We should be able to find unity around this center without a crushing uniformity which disallows any diversity in lifestyle, gifts, personality, practice, and beliefs outside the core. Our unity must be in a genuine

commitment to Christ, an open and honest search for His will for ourselves and each other, and a love for those whose faith is expressed in ways different from our own." (Leslie Woodson. *The Church United or Untied?* The Zondervan Corporation, Grand Rapids. Copyright, 1974 128).

We should know that our brothers and sisters meeting under different names or no name at all will always have theological understandings of the Scriptures that differ. Part of the reason for this would be because of different levels of spiritual maturity in addition to the stream of teaching to which we may have been regularly exposed. This is why I believe we should all be willing to seriously and transparently pray prayers such as the following, which happens to have been so meaningful to me in my own spiritual journey to this day. Repeating again from chapter three Psalm 25:4,5 reads:

"Show me YOUR ways, O Lord; Teach me YOUR paths. Lead me in YOUR truth and teach me, for You *are* the God of my salvation; On You I wait all the day" (emphasis mine).

Note the words, **"Lead me in Your truth."** We do not need man's imagined truth, but God's truth which is plain and understandable in the written Word.

God allowed me to experience seminary life, and I have observed that abstruse theological deliberations, ingenious semantical ponderings, and a tendency to bend scripture to fit a particular denominational dogma, can lead down a trail that puffs up intellect to the extent that it departs from the **"simplicity that is in Christ"** (2 Corinthians 11:3). He has promised to teach us what we need to know if we are teachable.

This is an extremely vital key to spiritual progress—*teachableness*. Are we willing to admit our need to be kept by God and our part in this? Are we humble enough to recognize our brothers and sisters as equal members in the body of Christ? I pray that we will catch the vision of the Church, the present kingdom of God on earth, and as His living representatives we will avail ourselves of the opportunity to be His humble servants through the days of our short physical lives. If we don't do this we will stumble along with our routine of going to church, paying our tithes, and having little or no effect on the world around us.

The scripture above also includes the practical prayer, **"Teach me Your paths."** The truth is that God does have a planned *path* for each of us to walk each day of our lives. Being obedient to stay on that path is the way to experience righteousness, peace and joy in the fullness of the Holy Spirit.

The whole purpose of our existence as professed believers in Jesus Christ is to become like Him. As this happens we will enjoy not only unity with Him, but also unity with others in the body of Christ. This is His will. Just as Jesus and the Father are as one because of their perfect love relationship with each other, so we can experience likewise depending on our willingness to submit to Him in all things. Surely it is time and necessary for each of us to examine our hearts. It is of great importance that we commit to obey Him and move in the direction He is calling us as we pray and seek His face. If we obey the leading of the Holy Spirit and do our part by responding in faith, we will find this scripture to be wonderfully true:

"Draw near to God and He will draw near to you" (James 4:8).

Chapter 10
Kept by the Power of God
John 17:12

"While I was with them in the world, I kept them in Your name. Those whom You gave Me I have kept; and none of them is lost except the son of perdition, that the Scripture might be fulfilled."

We have talked about God's will to keep us through the dangers of exposure to this sin-laden world, and now we must find out how God is able to do it, and what the consequences are if we fail to submit in obedience to His will. Jesus talked about some of His followers who had been kept, and also about one who had been lost—Judas. This matter of being *kept* or not is obviously of very serious concern to Jesus because He emphasizes again, as He did in the previous verse that His disciples were **"kept...in Your name."**

A basic exegetical deduction would be: Any followers of Jesus who are *not* kept will not enjoy the unity of fellowship enjoyed by those who *are* kept as faithful members of the body of Christ. Taking the words of Jesus at face value simply implies there will be those who are not kept—one was lost. Otherwise, once again, the words of Jesus would have no logical or realistic purpose unless the implied warning was real. In other words, the need to be kept implies the very real possibility of not being kept. To say that such people were never true followers of Christ in the first place is a disingenuous tactic to avoid the reality of the obvious. One teacher has referred to those who are guilty of practicing *exegetical gymnastics* as those who have fallen into the trap of doing so in order to keep their preferential theology intact. We should always seek to apply sensible understanding to the language and meaning of words just as God has given them to us. The fact is, Judas was one who was not ultimately kept, which counters the false unscriptural eternal security teaching of "once saved, always saved," or, putting it in other words, absolutely automatic predetermined perseverance of the saints. Nowhere in the Bible do we find such a sentiment expressed! It is another trick of the enemy which produces unnecessary division in the body of Christ, and Satan has been using teachings such as this for a long time—over 400 years. Remember once again my short quote: *"We should never bend the Scriptures to fit our theology. We should bend our theology to fit the Scriptures."*

Long-time English pastor of Millmead Baptist Church in Guildford, Surrey, UK, and biblical scholar David Pawson writes about being honest with the Scriptures from the Book of Hebrews, and what some refer to as "problem passages":

"The so-called 'problem' in Hebrews concerns the suggestion that believers may fall away from faith in Jesus and not be saved on the final day. The best known of these warnings is found in Hebrews chapter 6. But the letter also includes several other severe warnings to those who drift away (see 2:1; 3:5-6, 12-14; 6:4-8, 11-12; 10:23-30, 35-39; 12:14-17).

"These verses represent a thread running all the way through the letter, which starts in chapter 2 with the words, 'How shall *we* escape if we neglect so great a salvation?" [emphasis by writer]. Every time I have heard that quoted, it has been quoted against sinners who are neglecting the Gospel. But the 'we' here refers to Christian believers. The writer is saying that all we need to do to get into danger is to neglect our salvation. Most churches have members who have drifted away.

"The theme continues with two passages in chapter 3, the long one in chapter 6, and another in chapter 10, which says, 'If we deliberately keep on sinning after we have received the knowledge of the truth, no sacrifice for sins is left..." This has led some commentators to conclude that the people in question were not believers at all. He must have been writing about non-believers who became interested in Christianity but didn't continue. After all, what about 'Once saved, always saved'? But the description in chapter 6 of the people who are in danger is surely a description of those who have been born again! The writer is talking to those who have been 'enlightened', who have 'tasted the heavenly gift', who have 'shared in the Holy Spirit', who have 'tasted the goodness of the word of God and the powers of the coming age.' I cannot fit any unbeliever into that description. In any other letter, these phrases would not even be questioned as a description of Christians" (David Pawson, *Unlocking the Bible,* HarperCollins Publishers, © David Pawson 2007 686-687).

So why was Judas not *kept*? He certainly had the opportunity to be *kept* just as the rest of the disciples, but there was something different about Judas. Even though he had participated in actual ministry when sent out by Jesus as part of the seventy (Luke 10:1-20), he became a *lost* person. Somehow, his relationship with Jesus must have become different from the other disciples. Some commentators think he must have had secular ideas along the line of high political hopes for dispelling the Romans from Israel and became discouraged when it didn't seem to be happening through Jesus. Along this line of thought it is also evident the eleven disciples and other followers of Jesus had similar aspirations.

But whatever it was that caused Judas to be influenced away from being a wholehearted devoted follower and believer in Christ, he obviously became one who was no longer in harmony with Jesus and the other original eleven disciples. Our Lord's prayer, **"Those whom You** [the Father] **gave Me** [Jesus]," indicates that Judas was one who was given to Jesus in like manner that the rest of the disciples were. But just as in Adam's case, we see the consequence of freedom of choice which was given to Judas and is given to all of us by God. For those who might object because of being exposed to hyper teaching on the sovereignty of God, we should understand that God in His sovereignty gave man the gift of free will and freedom of choice, which is evident throughout the Bible. Free will means free will! Choice means choice.

This thought came to me one day as I was meditating on the possibility of a once-true believer becoming a stranger to the things of God: *You cannot fall out of a tree unless you have been in it!* Judas definitely had a relationship with Jesus initially, but he fell out of that relationship. This is what the salvation experience actually is, an active relationship with God based on repentance, faith, and continual submission of our wills and obedience to the Lord as we fellowship with Him daily. Our salvation relationship with the Lord is not some kind of magical spiritual connection that keeps us forever attached to Him regardless of our choices. Galatians 5:4 says:

"You have become estranged from Christ, you who *attempt to* be justified by law; you have fallen from grace."

This scripture is not difficult to understand. Any attempt to be approved of God for eternal salvation based on anything other than the blood atonement of Christ, such as in this case self-effort in keeping the Law, is totally unacceptable to God. In fact, it would be like slapping God in the face. It would result in *falling* from the freely offered grace that has been provided for all who will believe (John 3:16, **"whoever believes,"** and who continue to believe). The fact that some former believers in the church at Galatia had become

"estranged from Christ" and **"fallen from grace"** clearly shows that grace is not irresistible. Respected biblical scholar David Pawson says, "Grace is not an irresistible force, it is an undeserved favor" (*www.youtube.com. Israel in the Book of Romans. Accessed 1-20-19).* Judas is an example of one who fell from the grace of God by choosing a rebellious pathway. Once again: *You cannot fall out of a tree unless you have been in it!*

Having written the above, I recognize there is an enigmatic element to the situation regarding Judas. Jesus knew that someone would have to be the one to desert Him when He said, **"that the Scripture might** [or would] **be fulfilled."** Someone would be the one whom the Scriptures prophesied concerning who would actually turn traitor to the One he formerly followed. A prophecy from the Old Testament is believed by most commentators to refer to Jesus' experience with Judas. It reads:

"Even my own familiar friend in whom I trusted, who ate my bread, has lifted up *his* heel against me" (Psalm 41:9).

Note the words of this prophetic Psalm that the one who would betray Jesus was **"a familiar friend in whom I trusted."** But Jesus knew from the early days who would betray Him. For in John 6:64 Jesus said, **"But there are some of you who do not believe." For Jesus knew from the beginning who they were who did not believe, and who would betray Him.** It seems as though Judas was perhaps thinking: I'll wait and see if this Jesus really has what is needed for deliverance from Roman oppression. So, although Judas was a **"familiar friend,"** Jesus knew shortly after choosing him that he was to be the betrayer.

Remember that none of the disciples had the indwelling presence of the Holy Spirit during the three years they spent with Jesus in ministry. Jesus said, **"He** [the Spirit] **dwells with you and will be in you"**

(John 14:17), which was a reference to the coming Day of Pentecost after Jesus' resurrection. During the three years with Jesus their *salvation* was based on their personal commitment to follow Him as their Lord. It was Peter who confessed in answer to Jesus' question, **"Also we have come to believe and know that You are the Christ, the son of the living God." Jesus answered them, "Did I not choose you, the twelve, and one of you is a devil?"** (John 6:69,70).

Was Judas included in Jesus' prayer that His disciples would be one in unity? Of course, Jesus would not desire Judas to go to Hell, so Jesus' prayer for unity could have applied to him if he would have had a surrendered heart. Jesus would have wanted him to willingly commit himself as a true disciple, but He would not attempt to force Judas to believe in Him. This is just as God now deals with all of us today who have come to Him freely of our own will as influenced by His grace. But the Scripture had to be fulfilled, and Judas chose his own destiny. If it had not been him it would have been someone else. Theologian J. Rodman Williams writes concerning the tragic end of Judas:

The case of Judas Iscariot is just that. Jesus in His prayer to the Father (John 17) says, "While I was with them, I kept them in thy name, which thou hast given me; I have guarded them and none of them is lost but the son of perdition" (v. 12). Judas was numbered among those "given" to Jesus by the Father; he was chosen by Jesus as the other eleven apostles were. But somewhere along the way Satan got to him: "the devil having now put into the heart of Judas Iscariot...to betray him" (John 13:2 KJV). Jesus did speak of Judas earlier as "a devil"—**"Have not I chosen you twelve, and one of you is a devil?"** (John 6:70 KJV). But he was a devil by defection from his earlier faith (as John 13:2 demonstrates).

That Judas became apostate is clear from the later words of Peter (after Judas' suicide) concerning the need to select another apostle "to take the place in this ministry and apostleship from which Judas turned aside [Gr. *parebe,* "by transgression fell" KJV], to go to his own place" (Acts 1:25). This sad record of Judas' life and death is a demonstration that even with Jesus' keeping and guarding (John 17) of those the Father had given Him, such a one could still defect and be lost (J. Rodman Williams. *Renewal Theology Vol 2*, Zondervan, 1996 128).

While we should obviously be concerned about our own salvation individually, we need to ask ourselves to what degree we are concerned about the eternal destiny of our fellow believers—not to mention those of our loved ones and acquaintances who may be headed for eternal loss. How much do we pray for our saved brothers and sisters to stay strong in the faith? Have we shed tears for some who have fallen aside and left the faith? The Apostle Paul agonized over such individuals when writing to the believers at Philippi:

"For many walk, of whom I have told you often, and now tell you even weeping, *that they are* the enemies of the cross of Christ: whose end *is* destruction, whose god *is their* belly, and *whose* glory *is* in their shame—who set their mind on earthly things...so stand fast in the Lord, beloved" (Philippians 3:18,19; 4:1).

Once again, there will be those who will suggest because of Calvinistic theological presuppositions that Paul is not talking about people who have been genuine believers but non-believers, or those who have only made mental assent to following Christ. For example:

"It is not likely that these people were simply pagans, of whom nothing much better was to be expected. Rather, they were probably professing Christians, but ones whose lives were so profligate that it was clear to Paul that they had never been regenerated" (*The Expositor's Bible Commentary— Abridged Edition: New Testament,* Zondervan, 1994 807).

However, this is purely assumption on the part of the writer, because the scripture does not state that it is "clear to Paul that they had never been regenerated." The most likely understanding of what Paul is referring to in view of the context of the whole epistle which is written to believers, is that Paul has shed tears for those who had at one time been accepted members of the Philippian Church who had now walked away from their former identification as believers. We could mention many sad examples of such individuals today. The whole of the surrounding context of verses 18 and 19 show clearly that Paul is writing to Christians and is concerned as to their spiritual state. The beginning of this letter also clearly identifies to whom it is addressed.

"To all the saints in Christ Jesus who are in Philippi, with the bishops and deacons" (Philippians 1:1).

When Paul writes, **"For many walk"** (Greek is present active sense and can be translated **"For many now are walking"**) and **"whose end is destruction"** he cannot be referring exclusively to the unsaved world, but to those who have changed positionally from what they were formerly. The **"end"** of those who are not believers will obviously be destruction, and the same fate awaits those who have known the Lord but have apostatized and turned away from following Him by their own choices.

So, this is the challenge for all believers to strive through prayer for the answer to Jesus' prayer to become a reality. It is that the Church should be united in oneness. It is vital that as members of the body of Christ we pray fervently for all of us as individuals to submit and surrender our lives without reservation to the Lord. We should praise Him for His grace that is always available to keep us from turning away from the faith and continuing to maintain a relationship with Him. Unfortunately, Judas did not keep his relationship with Jesus with the sincerity of the other disciples and suffered the consequences.

So, what is God looking for? He is looking for a people who believe and trust Him totally and continue to develop a growing intimate relationship with Him of their own free will.

It is interesting, in the beautiful allegory of John Bunyan's *Pilgrim's Progress*, that at the end of *Christian's* journey Bunyan writes about one of *Christian's* companions named *Ignorance*:

> "His name was not found in the book of life…then I knew that there was a way to Hell from the gates of Heaven, as well as from the City of Destruction" (John Bunyan. *Pilgrim's Progress in Today's English*. The Moody Bible Institute, 1964 156).

Yes, we can be **"kept"** in relationship with Him if we joyfully submit to doing our part by trusting in His grace. What a joy it will be to have no regrets when we reach the end of our spiritual journey! In the next chapter we will discover how God can bless each of us with the joy of the Holy Spirit as we serve Him each day.

Chapter 11
Irrepressible Joy
John 17:13

"But now I come to You, and these things I speak in the world, that they may have My joy fulfilled in themselves."

At Christmastime Christians sing the carol, "Joy to the world! the Lord is come; let earth receive her King...Repeat the sounding joy." We often sing while at the same time being aware of the reality that the world is not full of joy. In fact, many times there are great tragedies that happen at this traditional time of the year, which often bring great sadness and loss to people in many parts of the world. Yet, the worldly parties continue unabated, and there is a kind of false, contrived, feigned joy based on the feelings of the moment which, of course, do not last.

It is sad and tragic to see people attempting to find some relief from the mundane routines of life only from things that stimulate them outwardly but do not spring from the heart. Some find temporary joy by turning to comedy (comedians are often the saddest and loneliest of people). Others think they will find satisfaction through alcohol or indulging in a variety of drugs and illicit sex. Even certain types of secular music can become addictive and not produce lasting contentment. The gift and purpose of music in its highest expression is for worshipping God. Another problem is the adulation of sporting heroes. Many may be guilty of making idols out of sporting events where for a brief time they often experience a level of outward happiness as they loudly express themselves. These are all examples of the ways people try to fill the vacuum that is within them. But there is a much better way.

In the scripture above we see that Jesus experienced joy. He had joy while knowing that in a short time He would be hung on a cross and experience excruciating pain and suffering before He died. In spite of the nearness of the crucifixion He had joy because He knew He was obeying the will of His Father. He wanted us to experience joy, not just any joy, but *His* joy: **"that they may have My joy."**

Can we begin to grasp the reality of this situation when Jesus uttered these words to His disciples? In a few hours He was going to experience such agonizing emotion and pain beyond what any of us will ever have to face in our lifetimes. He was the only one, the only Man on the face of the earth in the entire history of humanity, the only one who was worthy to meet and fulfill the just requirements of a holy God. He was literally to become, **"The Lamb of God who takes away the sin of the world"** (John 1:29). Yet, at this moment in time He was concerned that His disciples know for themselves the fullness of joy, **"fulfilled in themselves."**

Is there not an underlying commitment in the heart of Jesus causing Him to have perfect joy while knowing what was ahead for Him? How could Jesus talk of joy at such a serious time when He was facing the cross? John gives us the answer. Jesus declared, **"As the Father gave me commandment, so I do."** Yes, that is the secret which was open for all to see and understand. Jesus was submitted to the will of His Father. If we can get to the place individually where we can pray each day, "As you give me commandment, Father, so I will do," we will surely know by experience the inward joy that no one can take away. A prophetic Psalm that looks ahead to the ministry of Jesus reads, **"I delight to do Your will, O my God, and Your law is within my heart."** (Psalm 40:8). It is believed that Hebrews 10:5-7 picks up from this verse in the Psalms by further quoting:

"Sacrifice and offering You did not desire, but a body You have prepared for Me. In burnt offerings and sacrifices for sin You had no pleasure, then I said, 'Behold, I have come—in the volume of the book it is written of Me—to do your will, O God.' "

How foolish we are as we go through life if we do not develop this same commitment and attitude of obedience like Jesus. We have all been trapped and deceived into thinking we know best for the various situations we face in life. Many times, I have caught myself with this attitude until I remember to ask the Lord for His wisdom and submit to His will. Then the way is made clearer and things tend to fall into place. Joy is listed in Galatians 5:22,23:

"But the fruit of the Spirit is love, joy, peace, longsuffering, kindness, goodness, faithfulness, gentleness, self-control. Against such there is no law."

So, if we are indwelt by the Holy Spirit, we should be able to experience that which comes from the Spirit. But when we are careful to examine our lives and compare them to this list of the fruit of the Spirit, I confess that the challenge to trust God for these qualities to be evident in our lives on a consistent and regular basis is truly daunting. We can often go through the duties of the day and our interactions with people showing little faith, reliance, or submission to the Lord in order for Him to be able to manifest Himself through us in these ways. Paul wrote that these qualities are, **"the fruit of the Spirit,"** so if our lives are not giving witness to these things it must mean we are not in full fellowship with the Holy Spirit.

Why was Jesus concerned that we have His joy? Does this mean that we are to go around each day greeting people with a big smile on our face? Are we to use various other means of outward expression that might indicate to others we are always full of unending exuberance? Well, I am not opposed to smiles (you use fewer muscles smiling than frowning) because a smile can certainly be a pleasant thing to observe if sincere. But notice that Jesus said He wanted the disciples to have His joy **"in the world."**

Is it not true that our experiences in the day-to-day world can often drag us down spiritually and emotionally? When Jesus uttered the words of John 17:13 to His disciples, I doubt there was a big smile on His face. He was well aware of what they would soon face because of the traumatic reality of the cross, which would affect them to the core of their beings. So, although smiles are a pleasant thing to experience, there can be a much deeper sense of joy that is so real it will serve to steady and sustain believers both spiritually and emotionally.

Dictionaries tell us that joy is the pleasant emotion evoked by well-being, success or good fortune, or the thought of a desire to be fulfilled. I believe the quality of joy Jesus was talking about is something much deeper than what we generally think of as the kind of joy that is stimulated by outward experiences. As mentioned above, we may experience a level of happiness when we get excited about a sporting event. But such enjoyment is temporary and fleeting. The joy Jesus speaks about must surely be at a level and quality of meaningfulness that supersedes circumstantial surface joy and is more than outward stimulation.

In Luke 10:17-21 we see Jesus rejoicing with joy after He had sent 70 of His followers out for ministry. Luke writes:

"Then the seventy returned with joy, saying, 'Lord, even the demons are subject to us in Your name.' And He said to them, 'I saw Satan fall like lightning from heaven. Behold, I give you the authority to trample on serpents and scorpions, and over all the power of the enemy, and nothing

shall by any means hurt you. Nevertheless do not rejoice in this, that the spirits are subject to you, but rather rejoice because your names are written in heaven.'

"In that hour Jesus rejoiced in the Spirit and said, 'I thank You, Father, Lord of Heaven and Earth, that You have hidden these things from *the* wise and prudent and revealed them to babes. Even so, Father, for so it seemed good in Your sight.' "

What was it that caused Jesus to rejoice so openly after the 70 came back from their successful ministry? I suggest it was partly because His followers, including the twelve original disciples, were excited about being personally involved in the work and ministry of the kingdom of God. However, the fact that their names were written in heaven should have given them the greatest joy. Also, they were excited because they had seen the powers of darkness defeated. All of this was cause for great rejoicing to these early followers of Jesus then, but can be experienced today by all sincere Christians if we are willing to stay close in relationship with the Lord and dedicated to involvement in the work and ministry of the kingdom of God.

After this event of the 70 going out to minister as a team, we do not see any competitive spirit arising among these early disciples. They realized that their success was totally dependent upon their relationship with Jesus. It was through Him they experienced the power to heal the sick and deliver the oppressed from the clutches of Satan. They reported, **"Lord, even the demons are subject to us in Your name"** (Luke 10:17). There was no hint of personal achievement by any of them; they all knew it was by the **"name"** of the One they were following. What a lesson for us to remember when the enemy tries to get us to feel that *we* have accomplished something for the kingdom of God by our own merit!

We should all be challenged if we examine our daily lives honestly and discover the joy of Jesus is missing or lacking. When an unbeliever enters most churches today, will he or she sense the joy of the Lord in the atmosphere and expressions of the congregation as they worship? Why would an unbeliever be attracted to come back if there was no evidence that the people were enjoying their worship? And would there be anyone to greet them and tell them they were glad they were there?

These are some of the reasons why it is so important to know the joy of the Lord deep within our inner beings. It will be a great help to provide the foundation for unity in the body of Christ. How can there be real unity in the absence of joy and the other qualities of the fruit of the Spirit? And this joy will only come as individual believers are submitted and committed to an intimate relationship with the Holy Spirit.

Did you notice that in the scripture from Luke 10 above, it says Jesus rejoiced? He immediately began to thank the Father. He gave the Father glory and praise for the ministry that had been accomplished and for the experiences gained by the disciples. Jesus put into practice these words He knew from the Scriptures:

"Let all those who seek You rejoice and be glad in You. And let those who love Your salvation say continually, 'Let the Lord be magnified!' " (Psalm 70:4).

There is no competition in the combined divine Godhead of Father, Son, and Holy Spirit. There should be no competition among believers engaged in the work of God. If there is, it means there is a lack of maintaining the close intimate relationship with the Lord all of us are responsible for individually.

As just expressed, this is the answer to experiencing the joy of the Lord. Each of us as individual believers must keep close to the Lord through prayer and by delighting in the Word of God daily. If we do, we can have the deep joy of Jesus that will be a powerful witness to those we interact with each day. We can even have this joy in the midst of the most difficult and tragic experiences. In fact, James encourages us to **"Count it all joy when you fall into various trials, knowing that the testing of your faith produces patience** [endurance]" (James 1:2,3). I hope you are blessed with the joy of Jesus in your life, because this is what He wants for you. Here is a scripture to encourage us:

"I will greatly rejoice in the Lord, my soul shall be joyful in my God; for He has clothed me with the garments of salvation, He has covered me with the robe of righteousness" (Isaiah 61:10).

Having the joy of the Lord will also be a great witness to unbelievers as we are able to share with them the wonderful good news of the Gospel. May we all have the joy of the Lord today.

Chapter 12
Expect Hatred
John 17:14-16

"I have given them Your word; and the world has hated them because they are not of the world, just as I am not of the world. I do not pray that You should take them out of the world, but that You should keep them from the evil one. They are not of the world, just as I am not of the world."

Religious groups encountering others with differing theological beliefs, subjective opinions, and conflicting viewpoints is, of course, something common to church history. Time and history have repeatedly proven that in general people cannot get along with one another while living on this still beautiful but fallen planet. This unhappy historical scenario was initiated from the beginning of creation through the sin of Adam and Eve in the Garden of Eden. I wonder about the conversation that must have taken place between Adam and Eve after their banishment from that beautiful place.

The continuing unhappy and sorrowful state of this world because of sin in the heart of man was sadly prophesied by Jesus when He said, **"And you will hear of wars and rumors of wars"** (Matthew 24:6). People can differ so violently in their beliefs and ideologies even to the extent of killing one another by the millions. The twentieth century is considered by many historians to have been one of the most evil and devastating experienced by humanity. Millions of innocent people were literally murdered by dictators like Stalin (750,000 political opponents executed, plus a million sent to concentration camps), Hitler, (up to ten million executed), Pol Pot (two million died of starvation and execution), Idi Amin, (300,000 massacred), not to mention the two world wars plus Korea, Vietnam and others.

Not only do we see this miserable record of evil at a level of great distress among nations, but Jesus prophesied about the spiritual disruption which would also affect people at their personal levels as individual families when He said:

"For I have come to 'set a man against his father, a daughter against her mother, and a daughter-in-law against her mother-in-law'; and 'a man's enemies will be those of his own household.' He who loves father or mother more than Me is not worthy of Me. And he who loves son or daughter more than Me is not worthy of Me" (Matthew 10:35-37).

As Christians, we must accept the reality that many people in the unbelieving world are not going to be excited about our existence. In fact, as I write this, we are seeing Christianity and the Bible increasingly marginalized out of the public square in America, especially in the political and educational worlds. There is a satanic spiritual warfare that has been unceasing since Adam and Eve's failure in the garden. For those with spiritual discernment, it is clear that America is experiencing a fierce battle for the preservation of the biblical foundation and principles upon which she was founded.

But today's spiritual warfare is not just between Christians and non-Christians, but also, is sadly found among those who profess to be followers of Christ. This must surely be deeply grieving to the heart of God because the strength and witness of the Church as a whole is only made most effective by our oneness and unity in Him. Division and strife among the saints only generate unprofitable testimony to the world. Jesus repeatedly emphasized the importance of unity founded on genuine love. He said:

"A new commandment I give to you, that you love one another; as I have loved you, that you also love one another. By this all will know that you are My disciples, if you have love for one another" (John 13:34,35).

Brother against brother and sister against sister is obviously not going to get us anywhere that will provide effective ministry and bring glory to God. There has been a steady increase in America (over at least the last 60 years) of evolutionary-influenced college and university students becoming antagonistic to the beliefs of their parents—often to the parents' surprise, shock, and distress. The typical response of a twenty-first century university student when asked if they believe in evolution is, "Of course I do!" The connection between the influence of teaching evolution and aversion to biblical truth is clear for the discerning to see. Foundationally, if evolution is true there is no God who created all things. This is an obvious attack on the Book of Genesis which is the foundational book of the whole Bible.

The prophecy of Jesus is true. We are seeing breakdown of relationships between parents and their children. So-called modern progressive society has molded people in ways that tend to cause the destruction of relationships both individually, nationally, and internationally. Progressive ideology, instead of producing harmony and loving relationship among humanity, has certainly not helped to reduce conflict and hatred.

In the religious world, after someone has been deceived spiritually by false teaching and doctrine, it is very difficult for such a person to admit that what he or she has been taught and believed may be wrong. Human pride enters in and can very easily harden hearts even more, which will only cause the situation to get worse. How true it is that we are so often our own worst enemies because in our pride we are not willing to be told or corrected. Proverbs 12:15 says it plainly: **"The way of a fool *is* right in his own eyes. But he who heeds counsel *is* wise."** A spirit of humility is needed if there is any hope for oneness, but many times such a spirit will tend to remain elusive. A willingness to first be corrected by God and His Word would be the prerequisite for moving ahead in unity.

God has given humanity great gifts of ingenuity and creativeness because we are created in His image. But depending upon the influences we are exposed to individually and nationally, there are many ideologies that are diametrically opposed to one another. For example, we could learn a lesson from the past example set by those representing the original American colonies at the first Continental Congress. These original colonies were quite independently minded, especially religiously. When America's Founding Fathers representing these colonies were about to begin work on the Declaration of Independence from Britain, it was suggested that prayer be offered to seek God's divine aid. But right away there was a problem. American historian David Barton writes:

> On September 5, 1774, forty-five delegates gathered in Philadelphia in what became known as the First Continental Congress... As the delegates met one another and contemplated their course of action, John Adams reported their very first proposal after organizing themselves:
>
> *When the Congress first met, Mr. [Thomas] Cushing [of Massachusetts] made a motion that it should be opened with prayer.*
>
> This apparently harmless suggestion met unexpectedly stiff resistance:
>
> *It was opposed by Mr. [John] Jay of New York and Mr. [John] Rutledge of South Carolina because*

we were so divided in religious sentiments-of-some Episcopalians, some Quakers, some Anabaptists, some Presbyterians, and some Congregationalists—that we could not join in the same act of worship.

Strikingly, both opponents (Jay and Rutledge) were devoted Christians...these pious individuals opposed an opening prayer because the various delegates came from many different Christian denominations. (*The Founders' Bible,* Shiloh Road Publishers, LLC, Newbury Park, CA, 2012 828).

However, all was not lost, for eventually the delegates came together in agreement and asked Episcopalian minister Jacob Duché to be their chaplain and lead them in prayer. Thus, the need for unity enabled the representatives from those first thirteen colonies to cooperate and proceed with the task at hand. This was a victory in and of itself for the Founders to come together in agreement *in spite of their theological differences.* Somehow the Holy Spirit was able to diminish their strong feelings of denominational adherence and separation, bringing them to a sense of unity and purpose. They began to see the big picture of the watershed moment of American history in which they were privileged to be a part. They were being persecuted by the King of England. Will it take more persecution in the twenty-first century before Christians come together in unity and spiritual renewal?

We should learn the lesson from our Founding Fathers that God's divine overall purpose and plan for nations and individuals should always be considered as the highest priority—not what we want, but what God knows is best. It is one thing, sadly, to experience strong feelings of opposition to our own brothers and sisters in the faith when we are commanded to love one another, but another to know that we may be literally hated with demonic fervor by those who are walking in spiritual darkness. When the enemy, Satan, gets influence at the political governmental level of a nation, even in the Judeo-Christian founded nation of America, the Bible explains it vividly: **"When the righteous are in authority, the people rejoice; but when a wicked man rules, the people groan"** (Proverbs 29:2). Jesus warned us this would be the case and we should be prepared for it.

Therefore, the prayer of Jesus in John 17 regarding the persecution of His followers is becoming more obvious as we proceed through the days of this twenty-first century. We will be opposed and hated, yes, and not surprisingly this is actually happening today and increasing in what some are now calling post-Christian America. But as followers of Jesus Christ we know we are called to a unity that should be a clear witness to the secular world around us. For Christians to follow the example of our Founding Fathers, we should examine ourselves to see if our particular denominational beliefs put us beyond the possibility of uniting together with other sincere brothers and sisters for the furtherance of the kingdom of God. The question is: Are we willing to be this transparent before the Lord?

God's enemy is very active and, I believe, has a special hatred of America because of its Christian founding. There is a spirit of anti-Christ that has invaded many areas of our society—especially the political and educational worlds. Therefore, it is important to recognize the source of our opposition, particularly when it comes to opposition against anything to do with God, His Word, our teaching and preaching, and our relationship with other believers. The Bible makes clear that there are evil, unseen but very real, supernatural entities and influences to contend with. The problem we see taking place in the Garden of Eden was Eve's ignorance of the spiritual source and the consequences of believing the seductive voice she was hearing. So, from the very beginning of humanity we see that Satan succeeded in destroying the perfect unity that had been Adam and Eve's experience as husband and wife before the fall. Again, one can only imagine the conversations they must have had together after God compelled them to leave that beautiful environment of the garden. They were literally and physically transferred from a place of idyllic perfection and relationship with their Creator to the dreadful stark reality of a fallen world.

Opposition and almost any kind of confrontations with others are not situations the average person enjoys. So, one of Satan's ploys in order to discourage Christians from witnessing would be to try and discourage them from involvement in such encounters with those opposed to the Gospel. But Jesus made it clear that as His followers we are expected to spread the truth of the Gospel regardless of whether in friendly or antagonistic environments. If they had not been willing to do this in the past, there would have been no missionaries who sacrificed by leaving the familiarity of their homes and countries to go to other lands at the risk of their lives. Jesus said:

"Assuredly, I say to you, there is no one who has left house or brothers or sisters or father or mother or wife or children or lands, for My sake and the gospel's, who shall not receive a hundredfold now in this time—houses and brothers and sisters and mothers and children and lands, with persecutions—and in the age to come, eternal life" (Mark 10:29,30).

Why are Christians maligned and persecuted by those who tell us we must be tolerant of their beliefs, but at the same time are not tolerant of Christian teachings? It is obviously a contradictory and hypocritical stance, but they seem blind to their duplicity and double-dealing. Let's never forget, we are in a spiritual warfare and the enemy is not in the least interested in fairness—far from it! People are deceived, even willingly deceived, because they don't want to admit there is a holy, righteous God. Their sin nature wants complete control over them and they are like pawns in the destructive hand of the devil and his cohorts.

This reminds me of the blind hatred resident in the hearts of the Pharisees and Sadducees when they cried out for Jesus to be crucified. Dare I suggest that some professed Christians may be guilty of exhibiting similar attitudes to those of different denominational groups? Sadly, yes. For such a scenario to take place a lot will depend on how a professed Christian is hearing or not hearing from the Lord to sense His desire for love and unity among His people. Having a submissive spirit before the Lord concerning all the challenges of Christian relationships is absolutely needful. If one's personal relationship with the Lord is not as it should be, the unpleasant side of the sinful nature can easily show itself. The Bible says through the inspired pen of the Apostle Paul:

"Do you not know that to whom you present yourselves slaves to obey, you are that one's slaves whom you obey, whether of sin *leading* to death, or of obedience *leading* to righteousness?" (Romans 6:16).

It starts with a choice, **"to whom you present yourselves,"** and those who choose the evil way will walk in darkness and personal deception. But for the person who has become a believer Paul writes:

"For just as you presented your members *as* slaves of uncleanness, and of lawlessness *leading* to *more* lawlessness, so now present your members *as* slaves of righteousness for holiness" (Romans 6:19).

In the Garden of Eden Adam and Eve felt very comfortable in the presence of a righteous God, but after they sinned they hid from Him in fear. They no longer felt love, peace, joy or comfort in the presence of God. Their shield of innocence and purity was gone. Their sin had erected a spiritual barrier. In other words, we would say today that they were experiencing the convicting influence and power of the Holy Spirit. This is what unsaved people *should* experience when around believers today, but if professed believers are not filled with the Holy Spirit there will be no sense of conviction on the part of unbelievers.

Let us come to the reason Christians are hated by non-Christians. In our chapter verse above Jesus said that His disciples were hated **"because they are not of the world."** What does this mean? It must mean that those who have a personal relationship with God through Jesus Christ by the Holy Spirit, are living in a different dimension spiritually—even though still in the world physically. It means that if we are walking with God in holiness as we should be, we are covered and carry with us the influence of God's righteousness. In other words, as Christians we are to be in close intimate fellowship with God, and Jesus recognized this difference and distinction when He also said, **"They are not of the world, even as I am not of the world."**

So, there should obviously be a distinct difference in beliefs, attitudes, and general lifestyles and world views evident between believers and unbelievers. Therefore, it should be no surprise that unbelievers strongly influenced by the worldly spirit will often look at believers with an attitude of condescension, disdain, distrust, dislike, and even hatred. Unfortunately, professed believers who are not living with a close relationship with the Lord can also fall into this trap by criticizing and defaming other believers.

We see this scenario in the experience of the early disciples during a great time of ministry taking place by the power of the Holy Spirit that was having tremendous influence in Jerusalem. Thousands had come to faith in Jesus Christ, including a great number of the priests, and **"through the hands of the apostles many signs and wonders were done among the people"** (Acts 5: 12). But this did not make others happy. In fact, the Jewish high priest and other religious leaders with him were **"filled with indignation"** (Acts 5:17). After putting the apostles in prison, which didn't work as they hoped because **"an angel of the Lord opened the prison doors and brought them out"** (Acts 5:19), the angry religious leaders literally beat them physically—probably with rods—and **"commanded that they should not speak in the name of Jesus, and let them go"** (Acts 5:40).

After this shameful and unjust physical persecution (which is the kind of thing the devil delights in), we read that the disciples **"departed from the presence of the council, rejoicing that they were counted worthy to suffer shame for His name. And daily in the temple, and in every house, they did not cease teaching and preaching Jesus *as* the Christ"** (Acts 5:41,42).

I believe that this period of suffering for the sake of the Gospel in the lives of these early disciples would have surely had the effect of bonding them closely to each other in a loving unity. Unity such as they had not experienced at this level before this time. Dare I say that this may be just the thing that is needed in America among Christians today? Naturally we don't like the idea of it, but many have said that when real persecution comes to this country, then we will see the true Church rise together in loving unity and service to the Lord.

I don't believe the following true incident could hardly be called persecution. A man came into our Branson museum one day, and we asked him if he believed in a Creator God, which is what we normally ask our visitors to help us understand something about their background beliefs. He quickly said, "No." When I explained to him that our museum highlighted real science to support the history of the Bible he said, "If this is a religious thing I'm out of here." So, he left without being willing to take the guided tour through the museum. He is an example of the anti-God, anti-Bible spirit so prevalent in the world. This is the type of thing we may be faced with today. But I would not call these types of opposition real persecution. However, there has already begun to be milder cases of persecution happening in America that can be seen as the precursor to more difficult days ahead. If such comes and drives us into loving unity as brothers and sisters in Christ, I would have to think of this as a good thing.

Jesus said in our chapter verse that His followers are **"not of the world."** When fellow believers meet for the first time there should generally be a sense of belonging to one another because we have all partaken of the same Holy Spirit. We are **"not of the world,"** but we are part of the special spiritual world of those who have experienced the grace of God and forgiveness of sins through faith in Jesus Christ.

However, we have unfortunately heard the criticism that many professed Christians live a lifestyle that shows no distinction at all from those who are not believers. It is no wonder that unbelievers might observe the Church in general and be put off from being involved or connected. Also, if there is so much obvious division among Christians that they cannot agree with one another, as evidenced by the separate church buildings isolated from one another by short distances within a city, such a confusing visible testimony would naturally tend to discourage thinking unbelievers from having any personal connection. So, this is a problem that needs to be overcome with the help of the Lord. Yet, Jesus said it is by the testimony of our oneness that the world will believe.

In spite of how the world treats us because we are Christians let us determine with God's help to do as Jesus exhorts us:

"You have heard that it was said, 'You shall love your neighbor and hate your enemy.' But I say to you, love your enemies, bless those who curse you, do good to those who hate you, and pray for those who spitefully use you and persecute you, that you may be sons of your Father in heaven" (Matthew 5:43,44).

Chapter 13
Purity is Vital
John 17:17-19

"Sanctify them by Your truth. Your word is truth. As You sent Me into the world, I also have sent them into the world. And for their sakes I sanctify Myself, that they also may be sanctified by the truth."

"Pursue peace with all people, and holiness, without which no one will see the Lord: looking carefully lest anyone fall short of the grace of God; lest any root of bitterness springing up cause trouble, and by this many become defiled" (Hebrews 12:14,15). **"But as He who called you is holy, you also be holy in all your conduct, because it is written, 'Be holy, for I am holy' "** (1 Peter 1:15,16).

Sanctification and holiness. *Sanctification* means to be set apart and uniquely related to God in the spiritual dimension, and through this spiritual connection our outward lives should reflect this relationship in what would be seen as *holiness*. Why is this important? It is important because this is the will of God for His people. God would not be God, or at least not a good righteous God, unless His nature and attributes were perfect. As Christians, we are likewise called and commanded to be holy and righteous, first within our inner beings, our spirit/soul persons (sanctification), and then by demonstrating purity of living through our outward daily lives (holiness).

For a Christian today, especially in this twenty-first century where the pull of the secular world with its powerful temptations is so easily accessible, holiness of living may often seem like a goal unlikely to be reached.

In fact, if we allow ourselves to *think* such a goal is completely unattainable, we will not be encouraged to seek it through prayer and faith. If we should find ourselves in this undesirable state, we need to begin to correct our thinking and come into agreement with the Word of God. What the Bible clearly says is our absolute authority and standard for the way we live. If the Bible teaches the possibility of living a holy life, then it must be attainable. We need to make sure we are aligning our thinking, praying, testimony and confession of faith, with what God's Word teaches.

For example, since the Bible tells us Christ's presence lives within us as believers, we should have confidence and faith to know that all the resources we could ever need are available for us through the indwelling of Christ. The Apostle Paul emphasizes this when he wrote, **"that Christ may dwell in your hearts through *faith*"** (Ephesians 3:17, emphasis mine).

We must not forget the all-important ingredient of faith. If we truly believe this, that the presence of Jesus is within us through the ministry and filling of the Holy Spirit in our inner beings, such knowledge of this reality should literally affect every moment of our daily lives. All five senses of our physical bodies will be affected and should be under the influence of our Lord's presence within us. In our looking, our hearing, our smelling, our tasting, and our touching, all should be influenced by the Lord's presence within us. This gets right down to where we live and how we react to the world around us.

From the scriptures at the beginning of this chapter we notice this important statement Jesus made in His prayer for the disciples: **"Sanctify them by Your truth."** Since Jesus prayed this prayer for His disciples, it must certainly be a possibility in real-life experience. He would never have prayed this request of the Father for His disciples if it could not become a real experience in their daily lives. Was His prayer answered?

I believe we can see the answer in the plain fact of recorded history that these early disciples were willing to physically lay down their lives for Him. They literally separated themselves from anything that would hinder a holy relationship with their Lord. Even when they were faced with problems causing some to get emotionally hot under the collar (we could say unsanctified) about difficult issues (see Acts 15), they managed to come back under the unity of the Holy Spirit until peace reigned among them.

Since Jesus makes it clear that becoming sanctified as a believer is His will and a definite possibility, how is this to be accomplished? He gives a clear answer. He prayed that it is, "**by Your truth. Your Word is truth.**" Think about this for a moment. At the time Jesus prayed this prayer for His disciples the written *Word* to them was limited to the Old Testament. Was there enough teaching in the Old Testament to aid these disciples in becoming sanctified? There certainly is informationally, but something extra is needed for New Testament saints to bring this about in their personal experience. We see the answer in John 17:14 previously quoted in chapter six where Jesus said, **"For I have given them the words which You have given Me."** It is the Spirit-inspired teaching of Jesus Himself, *added* to the Old Testament truths along with the baptism of the Holy Spirit at Pentecost, that gave the disciples the extra inner strength needed to be able to live holy lives.

Think, for example, of the awesome teaching of Jesus we refer to as the Sermon on the Mount in Matthew's Gospel chapter five. The standard of living taught by Jesus seems so high and out of reach for imperfect people to attain. But the combination of Old Testament truths along with Jesus' teaching and the indwelling power of the Holy Spirit provides abundant divine provision and possibility for holiness and sanctification.

Jesus also said, **"The words that I speak to you are spirit, and *they* are life."** The words of Jesus in the spiritual realm contain the awesome power of creation. Jesus is the Creator. After all, John wrote, **"All things were made through Him, and without Him nothing was made that was made"** (John 1:3). We note that in the Book of Genesis when God *said* **"Let there be light"** (Genesis 1:3), the power of His creative words immediately brought light to bear on the incipient planet Earth (this was apparently the light of God Himself who is light—the sun not being created until day four of the creation week).

In the New Testament when Jesus *said* to the man with the withered arm **"Stretch out your hand"** (Matthew 12:13), the miracle of healing and complete wholeness happened instantaneously. Now, suppose the man with the withered arm had not obeyed Jesus and remained motionless, he would not have been healed. There must have been a degree of faith and hope in this man's mind and heart to lead him to follow the instruction of Jesus and make the conscious effort to stretch out his arm.

What does all this tell us related to holiness and sanctification? Simply put, it is to help explain something that is manifestly spiritually mysterious. It is *active faith in the living Words of God that activates His power.* The lesson to learn is that we must *believe* in the presence and power of God working within us and through us. We must *believe* that we can live a sanctified and holy life if we are to experience such victory. We must keep control of our thinking so that the influence of the world, the flesh and the devil cannot drag us down to the level of doubt and unbelief. We must *believe* that we can indeed be **"strong in the Lord and in the power of His might"** (Ephesians 6:10). We must *believe* that we can **"be strengthened**

with might through His Spirit in the inner man, that Christ may dwell in your [our] **hearts through faith"** (Ephesians 3:16,17).

If we *believe* His Word and know by faith that the living presence of Christ and the Holy Spirit dwells within us, we should realize there is potentially no lack of any provision for living a holy life pleasing to God. It depends on whether or not we commit to believe, just like those individuals recorded in the Gospels who were physically healed because of their faith. God has provided all we could ever need if only we will believe. David expressed this kind of faith when he wrote, **"The Lord is my shepherd; I shall not want"** (Psalm 23:1). He believed in the all-sufficiency of his all-providing Shepherd. After all, what does **"I shall not want"** not cover within the boundary of His will?

Returning to our chapter's first verse, it is **"by the truth"** if we commit to believing the Word that makes possible our sanctification. Is not such sanctification desperately needed in the body of Christ in order for harmony and unity to prevail among the various denominational and independent assemblies (Greek—*ekklesia)* of God's people? We now must ask ourselves a crucial and penetrating question: Are we willing to let the truth that can sanctify us work within us to achieve the results desired by God and the Holy Spirit? God will not force Himself upon us. But if *we* are willing, God is always willing. It will likely be a humbling and purging experience for most of us, but the rewards will be great if we let the Holy Spirit have His way.

Jesus is, of course, always our perfect example. He prayed, **"And for their sakes I sanctify Myself"** (John 17:19).

Question: Now why would the perfect, sinless Son of God need to sanctify Himself? He says that it was **"for their sakes."** So, Jesus demonstrated before His disciples how to be sanctified, or, another way of putting it, how to keep spiritually separated and holy in an unholy world. Obviously, Jesus Himself had no sin to be separated from. Biblical scholar Donald Stamps puts it well:

> "Jesus sanctifies himself by setting himself apart to do his Father's will and to accomplish the highest purpose for which he came to earth: to die on the cross and pay the price for our offences against God. Jesus suffered on the cross to restore the opportunity for people to have a relationship with God. Because of his personal sacrifice, Christians also are to separate themselves from the world and set themselves apart for God and his purposes" (Donald C. Stamps. *Fire Bible*. Springfield, MO: Life Publishers International, Study Notes, 2015 1505).

Each individual member of the body of Christ should be a powerful testimony and witness to the secular world by being seen and recognized as special and separate. Not by excessive difference of outward attire, but by the inward Spirit-filled temperament displaying the fruit of the Spirit for all to observe. Remember that Jesus said twice of His disciples, **"They are not of the world, just as I am not of the world"** (John 17:14,16).

The second verse quoted at the beginning of this chapter from Hebrews chapter twelve, gives us warnings to be aware of, which, if not taken seriously would destroy the possibility of spiritual oneness among God's people. In verse fifteen we read of one of these warnings, **"...lest any root of bitterness springing up cause trouble, and by this many become defiled."** The word **"bitterness"** (Greek—*pikria*) is akin to the emotion of hate, and anyone who yields themselves to such would only produce bitter fruit and disharmony with others. This would be in complete opposition to a sanctified life which should produce the beautiful and harmonious fruit of the Holy Spirit.

Sanctification and the manifestation of the love of God go together. Love should be the all-encompassing quality revealed through a sanctified life. It is no accident that *love* is at the top of the list of the fruit of the Holy Spirit: **"But the fruit of the Spirit is love, joy, peace, longsuffering, kindness, goodness, faithfulness, gentleness, self-control..."** (Galatians 5:22,23). And the Apostle Paul writes of three great Christian qualities with the most important one being love, **"And now abide faith, hope, love, these three; but the greatest of these *is* love"** (1 Corinthians 13:13).

We cannot be holy without the supreme inherent spiritual quality of love flowing from within by the Holy Spirit. I believe this is absolutely vital for us to reveal through our daily moment-by-moment lives with all sincerity. It takes us back once again to the foundation of the two great commandments. We are to love God with all of our being, and love those we interact with in our daily lives. Yes, we are even commanded to love our enemies (Matthew 5:43). True, this is not an easy mode of living for us to put into practice consistently and faithfully. For example, we all know by experience how difficult it can be to love someone with whom we feel a personality conflict.

So how do we get to the place where we love others as we should? The secret is definitely not to try to use our will power by sheer grit and determination, simply because we are commanded to do so. But by yielding to the Holy Spirit's fullness it is He who will then enable us to love both God and others through us. But after understanding this we will still need to know how to practically apply being sanctified and holy before the Lord. It is a matter of going back to the basics. The degree of sanctification we can experience will depend on our willing discipline and practical dedication to our devotional times of private prayer and feeding upon the Word of God. I cannot overemphasize how vital this is, because this is how faith develops and grows in strength. An evidence of this is shown by the enemy's constant attempts to keep us from being faithful to our private times of prayer and feeding on the living Word of God.

The Bible says, **"Pursue peace with all people, and holiness"** (Hebrews 12:14). It is up to us to determine how much we really want all these good things the Lord has for us. We are to **"Pursue...holiness"** intentionally. We should be saturating ourselves with the Scriptures by spending quality time in reading and meditation. Yes, it takes time, and in this day and age we can very easily say we just don't have time. But I believe it is a true sentiment that people *tend to find time for the things they really want to do.* They will make time to watch one of their favorite programs on TV. So many will limit the time of personal meaningful intimacy with the Lord because they give priority to other things which seem more pressing.

It is said of Enoch during Old Testament times that he **"walked with God"** (Genesis 5:24). If we are going to walk *with* God, we will obviously have to keep in step with Him. We would not want to lag behind or run ahead. So, once again, it is the daily, moment-by-moment living relationship and fellowship with the Lord that will yield holy and sanctified living. Something that should naturally follow such a lifestyle would be increased harmony and unity with our brothers and sisters in Christ. It begins with you and me and our personal relationship with the Lord. Are we willing to pay the price? The rewards will be great.

Chapter 14
We Are the Subjects of Prayer
John 17:20

"I do not pray for these alone, but also for those who will believe in Me through their word."

It is always extremely encouraging for Christians to know that others are sincerely praying for them. We all need to be encouraged as spirit/soul beings when we experience the outward ups and downs of life with its varying emotions and vicissitudes. From the very beginning of Christianity, the people of God have known how vital it is to maintain connection with their Father in Heaven through Jesus Christ, and prayer is the means God has provided.

He is the Creator of each one of us, and therefore cares deeply for us as individuals. This is one attribute that separates the true God from all imposters. He knows all about us and offers His love to all. Even as Christians, in what we might consider the less important matters to pray about, the Word of God encourages us to bring all our concerns to Him, and He will help us. For example, the Apostle Paul writes:

"Be anxious for nothing, but in everything by prayer and supplication, with thanksgiving, let your requests be made known to God; and the peace of God, which surpasses all understanding, will guard your hearts and minds through Christ Jesus" (Philippians 4:6,7).

If we are **"anxious for nothing"** (trusting without fear) we can pray in faith believing that God's help is on the way. Now I realize it is not always easy to keep anxiety out of our minds when faced with difficulties that can become extremely stressful and traumatic. We all need to have our hearts and minds guarded from the attacks of the evil one. But if we truly believe God is hearing our prayers, we can also help our faith along by doing what this scripture suggests, praying **"with thanksgiving."** In other words, giving thanks as we pray shows that we are putting our complete faith in Him, and believing that the answer to our prayers is assured. In fact, Jesus said, **"If you abide in Me, and My words abide in you, you will ask what you desire, and it shall be done for you"** (John 15:7). In other words, if we approach God in prayer the right way, we can believe we receive by faith with thanksgiving before the actual answer comes to pass in real time.

The Book of Acts records a situation that would have naturally caused extreme anxiety on the part of the early believers. The Apostle Peter had been arrested and put in prison by King Herod, and the outlook seemed very bleak because Herod was planning to execute Peter, just as he had recently put James the brother of John to death (Acts 12:2). But prayer intervened, and played an important part, arguably the most vital and crucial factor in Peter's deliverance. Acts 12:5 says, **"Peter was therefore kept in prison, but constant prayer was offered to God for him by the church."** After Peter was miraculously delivered from the prison, we read that he **"came to the house of Mary, the mother of John whose surname was Mark, where many were gathered together praying"** (Acts 12:12).

Of course, the believers were obviously praying that Peter would be spared the cruel ignominious death that appeared to be his fate. But in this case, I believe God used the prayers of the believers to intervene miraculously for Peter. Not only for Peter, but for all those who would be blessed by his ministry in the future.

Question: Would God have delivered Peter anyway regardless of whether he was prayed for or not?

I don't know. We have to recognize the overruling sovereignty of God in some situations, but I do know that we are exhorted to pray for one another. Obviously, this is because prayer offered in faith will produce results. Jesus himself exhorts us, **"In this manner, therefore, pray: Our Father in heaven..."** (Matthew 6:9).

Yes, it is comforting to know we are being prayed for, but how wonderful and awesome beyond words to know that the Lord Jesus Christ himself is praying for us! Look at the words of our chapter verse again:

"I do not pray for these alone, but also for those who will believe in Me through their word."

Does this truth humble you when you realize that the Creator of the universe is praying for you personally? Who would know better how to pray for us than the One who knows all about us and what we will face in life? Jesus knew that the Apostle Peter was going to be severely attacked by the enemy, and right before the crucifixion He said to him:

"And the Lord said, 'Simon, Simon! Indeed, Satan has asked for you, that he may sift you as wheat. But I have prayed for you, that your faith should not frail; and when you have returned to Me, strengthen your brethren' " (Luke 22:31,32).

It seems easy to forget the reality of the fact that God sees and knows everything. Nothing takes God by surprise. In 2 Chronicles 16:9 we read:

"For the eyes of the Lord run to and fro throughout the whole earth, to show Himself strong on behalf of those whose heart is loyal to Him."

Note the condition for experiencing God's power in our lives; **"those whose heart is loyal to Him."** If all these things are true regarding God's desire to help us through the challenges of life, we would be foolish beyond imagination to not avail ourselves and discipline ourselves to utilize these means of grace—namely, prayer, confession and faith in His Word.

As Christians today, we have believed on Jesus for salvation because we have been ministered to through the words of the original disciples. Although not hearing with our physical ears these words spoken two thousand years ago, we have them available today through the miraculously preserved written Scriptures, the Bible. When we spend time with the Word of God, we should realize the great privilege that is ours to have had these words of life preserved for us from which to benefit.

Through the power of the living Word we could give countless testimonies of transformed lives. An outstanding example from history would be John Newton, (1725-1807), who was a captain of one of those terrible African slave trade ships for ten years. He was converted, became a minister, and wrote the well-known hymn *Amazing Grace.* I want to share with you a lesser known hymn of Newton's, published in 1779, titled: *Quiet, Lord, my Froward Heart,* which reveals his total change of heart and commitment to the Lord.

"Quiet, Lord, my froward [wayward] heart;
Make me teachable and mild,
Upright, simple, free from art;
Make me as a little child—
From distrust and envy free,
Pleased with all that pleases Thee.
What Thou shalt today provide,
Let me as a child receive;
What tomorrow may betide,
Calmly to Thy wisdom leave;
'Tis enough that Thou wilt care—
Why should I the burden bear?

As a little child relies
On a care beyond his own,
Knows he's neither strong nor wise,

Fears to stir a step alone—
Let me thus with Thee abide,
As my Father, Guard, and Guide!

Thus preserved from Satan's wiles,
Safe from dangers, free from fears;
May I live upon Thy smiles,
Till the promised hour appears;
When the sons of God shall prove
All their Father's boundless love.
(Golden Bells, London. Novello & Co. 1925 328, public domain)

Can you imagine such a coarse, brutal slave ship captain so transformed as to write these transparently beautiful words? This gives evidence of the power of the Word of God at work in human lives. No psychologist can even begin to match the biblical wisdom that can be applied to those who submit themselves to its counsel. The Bible is not just ink on paper, but it has a supernatural ingredient to it that no other "religious" writing contains. A powerful verse reads:

"For the word of God *is* living and powerful, and sharper than any two-edged sword, piercing even to the division of soul and spirit, and of joints and marrow, and is a discerner of the thoughts and intents of the heart" (Hebrews 4:12).

Jesus is literally praying for us as we live our daily twenty-first century Christian lives. Just because our lives and the circumstances in which we find ourselves are quite different from life as it was in the first century and the centuries since, the Word of God is still applicable to all situations. When we realize that the added ingredient to the written Word of God is God the Holy Spirit Himself, we can begin to grasp why the Bible is so different from other spiritual writings. We should have no problem believing this scripture:

"*It is* Christ who died, and furthermore is also risen, who is even at the right hand of God, who also makes intercession for us" (Romans 8:34).

Or, this scripture:

"Therefore He is also able to save to the uttermost those who come to God through Him, since He always lives to make intercession for them" (Hebrews 7:25).

Not only does our Lord pray for us individually, but He prays for the Church corporately. The battle against evil continues in the heavenly realms to this day. The devil is still opposed to God in his rebellion, and still hopes that in some way he can thwart the eternal purposes of God and come out the victor. But, thank God, this is not going to happen! The final end of the devil and all his schemes is eternal destruction in the lake of fire.

"The devil, who deceived them, was cast into the lake of fire and brimstone where the beast and the false prophet *are.* And they will be tormented day and night forever and ever" (Revelation 20:10).

As Jesus prays for His Church, the end result will be victory. There will be millions, if not billions of those who are part of the fullness of the spiritual body of the Church, having gained personal victory over the enemy, and will find themselves enjoying the blessings of God for all eternity in His presence. Here are a few scriptures to confirm this:

"I thank my God always concerning you for the grace of God which was given to you by Christ Jesus, that you were enriched in every thing by Him in all utterance and all knowledge, even as the testimony of Christ was confirmed in you, so that you come short in no gift, eagerly waiting for the revelation of our Lord Jesus Christ, who will also confirm you to the end, *that you may be* **blameless in the day of our Lord Jesus Christ"** (1 Corinthians 1:4-8).

And:

"Now may the God of peace Himself sanctify you completely; and may your whole spirit, soul, and body be preserved blameless at the coming of our Lord Jesus Christ. He who calls you is faithful, who also will do *it***"** (1 Thessalonians 5:23,24).

Question: Am I as an individual Christian praying and trusting the Lord for my life to fill the part in the body of Christ that God has planned for me? Am I actually contributing to the unity of the Church through my life and testimony? Do I submit to God and His plan for me, even if it does not feel comfortable to me? Do I keep up my personal intimate relationship with Him through prayer and the Word so that I will hear and understand His direction for my life? Am I willing to take up my cross daily and follow Him, as Jesus said in Matthew 16:24?

This is the challenge we all face as Christians throughout every day of our lives. The pull of the world, the flesh, and the devil is very real and powerful. Our only hope for an eternally meaningful and purposeful life is to walk with the Lord as He leads us. We cannot live a life we will look back upon in the future with satisfaction unless our lives have been fruitful for Him and His purposes. I personally don't want to be guilty of wasting my life on that which is of no eternal value. I aim to always keep the most important things as the most important things.

As I have emphasized previously, love is the foundational key. May my heart's cry be the same as the Apostle Paul when he lovingly expressed his desire for the brothers and sisters in Christ when he wrote, **"Now** may the Lord make you increase and abound in love to one another and to all" (1 Thessalonians 3:12).

Chapter 15
Unbelievable Union
John 17:21

"That they all may be one, as You, Father, *are* in me, and I in You; that they also may be one in Us, that the world may believe that You sent Me."

I consider these words contained in the prayer of Jesus the foundational verse for this book. This is the vision I believe God has put on my heart, which is to see the people of God move ahead in unity of relationship with one another. As such happens, and I believe it must, would not the words "revival" and "spiritual renewal" come to mind? For surely real spiritual unity would cause new life and energy to emerge and flow in fellowships of Christians. This would strengthen the Church as a whole and increase the effectiveness of Gospel witness. Somehow, we must get to the place where our denominationally-minded exclusivity and our myopic, staunch adherence to questionable dogma become secondary to God's overall purpose for the Church. In the very beginning days of the Church we read these wonderfully inspiring words:

"These all continued with one accord (Greek—*homothumadon,* from two Greek root words meaning "same" and "mind") **in prayer and supplication ...(about a hundred and twenty)...When the Day of Pentecost had fully come, they were all with one accord** (Greek— *homou,* "together") **in one place"** (Acts 1:14,15; 2:1). Then we read how this unity of heart and mind continued after the Day of Pentecost from the words in Acts 2:46, and as yet no hint of doctrinal differences:

"So continuing daily with one accord in the temple, and breaking bread from house to house,

they ate their food with gladness and simplicity of heart, praising God and having favor with all the people."

However, it wasn't long before the enemy of God began to raise opposition to the disciples' ministry, so they resorted to united prayer as recoded in Acts 4:24,32,33), but still, no hint of doctrinal differences:

"So when they heard that, they raised their voice to God with one accord and said: 'Lord, You *are* God, who made heaven and earth and the sea, and all that is in them'...Now the multitude of those who believed were of one heart and one soul...and great grace was upon them all."

The enemy of God, Satan, began his attacks on the Gospel from the very beginning of the Church, and to this day is actively opposing all of God's work in every way he can. But in this spiritual warfare we are not left helpless—far from it. As the early disciples knew where to turn when faced with opposition, so we today have the same availability extended to us, and the same access to the One whose presence in us is greater than he (Satan) who is in the world (1 John 4:4).

The situation we face today is the result of Satan's work over the centuries in doing his best to keep believers from being together in **"one accord."** He is well aware of the fact that Christians in Holy-Spirit unity have tremendous access to the power of God, both for their individual lives and for the effectiveness of the Church as a whole. Jesus said:

"Again [most assuredly] **I say to you that if two of you agree on earth concerning anything that they ask, it will be done for them by My Father in heaven. For where two or three are gathered in My name, I am there in the midst of them"** (Matthew 18:19,20).

We should be thinking: How can we lose? With all the promised help guaranteed to us from the Lord, surely we should always be gaining victory after victory over the enemy and his cunning attacks. Yet, just as Jesus had to rebuke some of the early churches as recorded in the Book of Revelation, so today, I believe the Lord would have words of rebuke and correction for us. Unfortunately, so much of church ministry has been carried on with what has been thought of as necessary compromise by incorporating worldly methods. Why is it that we can be so easily intimidated by others, whether apparently well-meaning Christians or those with so-imagined secular wisdom, that we let the simplicity of following Christ and the Holy Spirit fade into subordinate influence?

As Christians, we need to take seriously the way God has provided for us to combat the enemy by individually believing and applying these words:

"Finally, my brethren, be strong in the Lord and in the power of His might. Put on the whole armor of God, that you may be able to stand against the wiles of the devil" (Ephesians 6:10,11).

We should remember that although Christians can become **"strong in the Lord"** spiritually and become victorious in many ways against the powers of darkness, there will be times when it seems as though the enemy has won. When King Herod killed James the brother of John, when Steven was martyred, and when the Apostle Paul was finally killed, it might give the impression that Satan was winning the battle. But actually, he was not, and will never be ultimately successful.

Although many individual Christians may die for their faith and are immediately ushered into the presence of the Lord—which is a blessing for them—history has shown that in times of persecution Church growth multiplies at a rapid rate. China is a typical example of this. Dying for love of God the Father and Jesus Christ is a privilege that all of us should consider seriously, and know that in the sovereignty of God He is in ultimate control. I will never forget hearing of

Chinese Christians who were weeping in prayer while being observed by missionary Dennis Balcombe. He thought they were weeping because of the persecution some of the members were experiencing, and I'm sure this was part of their concern. But to his surprise, Balcombe heard some of those praying saying, "Lord, why did you not let me be the one to suffer for you!" The Book of Hebrews refers to those who suffer for the cause of righteousness as individuals **"of whom the world was not worthy...having obtained a good testimony"** and that we should **"run with endurance the race that is set before us"** (Hebrews 11:38,39; 12:1).

Putting it simply, while the Lord gives us life, energy and time to serve Him, we should not be lackadaisical in our obedience to follow Him with all of the giftings and ability He has given us for service. The principle Jesus taught in one of His parables encourages us to, **"Do business (KJV- occupy) till I come"** (Luke 19:13). Even in the Garden of Eden Adam and Eve were to *occupy* themselves by tending and cultivating the garden (Genesis 2:15).

The prayer of Jesus should be easy to understand when He prayed, **"That they all may be one."** Some may respond by saying that we are already *one* because true believers have all partaken of the same Holy Spirit and salvation. Yes, in the spiritual sense we understand this to be true, but Jesus made it clear that our oneness was also to be a powerful witness to the world in a visible way. He said, **"that the world may believe that You sent Me."** The unsaved world will never fully understand our unity in Christ from a spiritual perspective, because their philosophy is opposite to the principle of faith: if I first see, then I will believe. The Apostle Paul wrote: **"But the natural man does not receive the things of the Spirit of God, for they are foolishness to him; nor can he know *them,***

because they are spiritually discerned" (1 Corinthians 2:14).

There is something much deeper in the matter of being one in Christ and being able to express this unity outwardly. It has to do with the spiritual foundation of our personal relationship with the Lord. Jesus tells us about this in the same verse when He prayed, **"...as You, Father, are in me, and I in You; that they also may be one in Us"** (John 17:21).

Some people might think of this as related to spiritual mysticism, and I can understand why. But as Jesus reveals these awesome truths it should thrill us in the depth of our beings beyond anything else that could excite us in life. Jesus is reminding us who have spiritual eyes to see, that just as the Apostle Paul recorded many times in his epistles, we are privileged to have the *very presence of almighty God dwelling within us.* A word study of the times Paul referred to himself and other believers as being **"in Christ"** is highly recommended and quite revealing.

One easy way to begin to understand this is that as humans in physical flesh we find that we can communicate with other humans in physical flesh through the gift of speech or even nonverbal communication. In another way at another level, since we are also beings with a spirit residing within us, it is possible for spirit to communicate with spirit. But on a physical level alone, such communication is obviously lacking in many ways. This is why so many disharmonies can develop among individuals who are spiritually carnal with no personal, intimate knowledge of God, and this can even extend to nations as a whole. Jesus predicted such disharmony with the words: **"And you will hear of wars and rumors of wars"** (Matthew 24:6).

In our scripture verse Jesus is actually saying that just as He was one in spirit with the Father, so the awesome truth is that He is actually residing *within us* as believers. Do we really believe this? I know as evangelicals we talk about asking Jesus into our hearts to be saved, but from that point on do we really acknowledge His actual living presence within us in the reality of daily living? This is why the Apostle Paul emphasized such an important truth with these words in his prayer for the Ephesian believers:

"That He would grant you, according to the riches of His glory, to be strengthened with might through His Spirit in the inner man, *that Christ may dwell in your hearts through faith*" (Ephesians 3:16,17, emphasis mine).

This is almost as if a secret which has not been emphasized and explained by preachers and teachers of God's Word as much as it should. Literally believing and being aware of Christ's spiritual presence by the ministry of the Holy Spirit is something I did not grasp for many years as a believer myself. Paul did his best to bring this truth home to believers through his writings over and over again. He tells the Colossian Christians about the glorious riches God has given them in a mystery that only believers are privileged to experience. He writes:

"I became a minister according the stewardship from God which was given to me for you, to fulfill the word of God, the mystery which has been hidden from ages and from generations, but now has been revealed to His saints. To them God willed to make known what are the riches of the glory of this mystery among the Gentiles: which is, *Christ in you*, the hope of glory" (Colossians 1:25 -27, emphasis mine)

This is the most amazing revelation that became known to the early Christians, and now known to us who have the privilege of having this information passed on to us through the Scriptures.

I have to ask you, my reader, a serious but exciting and momentous question: Have you really considered the awesomeness of this truth? Do you put into practice a reliance on the presence of Christ within you during your daily life and interaction with others? If this is something new for you to consider I would encourage you to spend time in prayer until the reality of this truth really comes home to you, and it becomes part of your experience.

I want to make clear at this point that I am personally still seeking to develop my faith in trusting for the fullness of His presence to be manifest in me daily. The implications are staggering. Would we like for our testimony to reveal more of the fruit of the Spirit in our daily discourse with others? I certainly would. Well, as believers we have the presence and unlimited resources of Jesus living within us. But this will only come to reality in our lives if we earnestly pray and believe in faith. Would we like our testimony and witness to include gifts of the Holy Spirit according to His will? We should all desire this just as the early disciples did. They wanted all God had for them in order to be the most effective influence they could be for the Gospel. They prayed:

"Grant to Your servants that with all boldness they may speak Your word, by stretching out Your hand to heal, and that signs and wonders may be done through the name of Your holy Servant Jesus" (Acts:4:29,30).

God answered their prayer and with great boldness and powerful demonstration of the Holy Spirit's gifts there were many coming to the Lord. How would faith in the real presence of Christ in a body of Christian believers affect their oneness and unity? I believe it would make tremendous difference. With the wisdom of Jesus dwelling in the hearts of the believers it would surely foster loving respect and a desire to submit to one another in the love of Christ.

We have not yet mentioned the part of our chapter verse that tells us why Jesus thought it so important that those who believe in Him should be united as one. He said, **"...that they also may be one in Us, that the world may believe that You sent Me."** Yes, the power of a united Church should be an awesome thing for the world to recognize and behold. Yet, as we know, this is in general exactly what they don't see. There will always be a lack of spiritual power when God's people are not united in Him. If the unsaved population in the world does not see any reason to believe that Jesus is special and unique, separate from all other religious leaders, and that He came from the unseen spiritual dimension onto this earth, they will be hindered from ever coming into a saving relationship with God. And God's ordained plan has always been for the unsaved to come to Him for salvation through the ministry of a united Church.

I think one of the highest rewards for any believer in this life, is to have someone who has recently become a believer say to them: "There was just something about you; I knew that I wanted what you have." What is it that the world will notice that is distinct about believers? It is the unnatural evidence displayed by the believer that there is something much more important in life than worldly interests. It is the evidence of a life exhibiting love, joy, peace, and the fruit of the Holy Spirit in all circumstances, even negative ones. And as Jesus said, it is the evidence of groups of people who can actually get along with one another in a loving spirit of harmony.

I could list many more characteristics of God's people, the Church, (Greek— *ekklesia*, called-out ones, an assembly of God's people) that should be *visible* outwardly. But the secret and ultimate source of all such godly behavior springs from that which is within and *unseen*. When Jesus said that if we as believers are **"one in Us,"** meaning that there is an unseen spiritual dimension where we are so intimately identified in oneness with the Father and the Son, that the unseen power of this connection will aid unbelievers to believe. They will more easily be able to believe for themselves that Jesus truly is who He said He is. In other words, there should be a spiritual unseen influence emanating from believers to the unbelieving world, and this will help persuade them to accept the reality of the one true God who wants to lovingly draw them into Himself and save them.

Of course, the only way for each of our personal Christian lives and testimonies to be used of God in this way is for each of us to be overflowing with His presence by the Holy Spirit. God's plan is for us to be filled with His Spirit (see chapter 22). Remember that the Apostle Paul prayed for the Ephesian believers that they would **"...know the love of Christ which passes knowledge; that you may be filled with all the fullness of God"** (Ephesians 3:19).

This brings to us the challenge of self-examination of our own relationship with God. If we are not filled with His presence our lives will not have the influence and effect upon others that is God's plan for our witness. We will either be enticed by all the distractions of life that hinder a close intimate relationship with God, or we will concentrate on that which is of eternal value. Paul wrote:

"See then that you walk circumspectly, not as fools but as wise, redeeming the time, because the days are evil. Therefore do not be unwise, but understand what the will of the Lord is. And do not be drunk with wine, in which is dissipation; but *be filled with the Spirit*" (Ephesians 5:15-18, emphasis mine).

I pray that all of us will make sure we are seeking, asking, and believing in prayer to be **"filled with the Spirit"** so that our lives will be the most effective for God's eternal purposes.

Chapter 16
The Purpose of Union
John 17:22,23

"And the glory which You gave Me I have given them, that they may be one just as We are one: I in them, and You in Me; that they may be made perfect in one, and that the world may know that You have sent Me, and have loved them as You have loved Me."

The Master Teacher knew very well the value of repetition when teaching truth. Here He goes over similar thoughts to His previous words with the additional idea of **"glory,"** and the astonishing request of the Father that his disciples **"...be made perfect in one."** We do not know what was going through the minds of the disciples as they were listening to the words of Jesus' prayer, but later they would remember them and record His words as we have them in the written Gospels.

Jesus said in His prayer that the Father had given Him **"glory,"** and now He was passing this **"glory"** on to his disciples. What exactly was the glory to which Jesus was referring? John gives us insight on the meaning of this when he wrote:

"And the Word became flesh and dwelt among us, and we beheld His glory, the glory as of the only begotten of the Father, full of grace and truth" (John 1:14).

And:

"This beginning of signs [water into wine] **Jesus did in Cana of Galilee, and manifested** [revealed] **His glory; and His disciples believed in Him"** (John 2:11).

There are many facets of possible meanings to consider when trying to explain what is meant by Jesus' use of the word **"glory"** (Greek—*doxa).* Spiros Zodhiates, a biblical scholar and commentator who happens to be of natural Greek ethnicity, and whom I have personally met writes:

"In the NT, the...concept of glory is seen in Luke's account of the nativity (Luke 2:9) and of the transfiguration (Luke 9:28ff.) where the glory of Christ shines forth visibly in the dazzling brightness of His countenance. It encompasses the forms of Moses and Elijah (Luke 9:30), and even transfigures material objects like Christ's clothing (Luke 9:29).

What is meant by the glory and the glorifying of Jesus Christ? It means the revelation of His essential deity, that which He is in the mind of the Father, though veiled from man by the limitations of the incarnation...When in John 17:1,5,24 the Lord prayed for His glorification by the Father, He was looking forward to the splendor of His passion as issuing in the resurrection, wherein His true nature and redemptive work are recognized and celebrated by the faithful." (Spiros Zodhiates, *The Complete Word Study Dictionary: New Testament,* AMG Publishers, Chattanooga, TN. 1992 480).

Zodhiates mentions the great hope of all Christians which is the resurrection of Christ, which also gives confident hope for the resurrection of all true believers. In Colossians 3:4 Paul shares this exciting truth: **"When Christ *who* is our life appears, then you also will appear with Him in glory."** Christians have this unique hope of experiencing a perfect glorified body for all eternity like the glorified body Jesus has had since His resurrection. Christians can also envision this glorious future scenario as described by the Apostle John:

"And God will wipe away every tear from their eyes; there shall be no more death, nor sorrow, nor crying. There shall be no more pain, for the former things have passed away" (Revelation 21:4). This will be glory indeed!

I believe one of the best ways to understand what *glory* means is to simply recognize that Jesus, as God, could do what no other could do. After all, as part of the Triune Godhead He is the omnipotent Creator of all life. When He changed the water into wine, demonstrated His power over sickness and disease, multiplied the loaves and fish, walked on water, etc., He literally demonstrated the glory of God by giving us a small glimpse into its reality. To experience God's *glory* is to know something of the heavenly dimension, which is totally, well, heavenly.

The incredible truth is that Jesus said He had given glory to His disciples, **"And the glory which You gave Me I have given them."** Is it not a glorious thing to know that a sinner far from God in the realms of spiritual darkness can be transformed into a follower of Christ with power and victory over the world, the flesh, and the devil? Yes, indeed. And Jesus was giving His disciples the supreme privilege of being the messengers of His glory for the salvation of those who would believe. Paul writes:

"God...has given us the ministry of reconciliation...Now then, we are ambassadors for Christ, as though God were pleading through us; we implore *you* on Christ's behalf, be reconciled to God" (2 Corinthians 5:18,20).

What a privilege is ours, what glory, for us to be given the sacred calling of being His instruments to convey the message of the truth of the Gospel to the unsaved. This is why it is so vital for the body of Christ to be a united body with harmony among its members, and to be seen as such in the eyes of the unbelieving world. Now, if each of us is honest as we examine our individual relationship with God, we may be tempted to think we are not able to reach these realms of glory in serving the Lord.

But the prayer of our Lord does not let us off the hook because He actually prays for us with this amazing request. He prayed, **"...that they may be made perfect in one."** Would Jesus pray for something that was not possible? Of course not! So, this is the challenge Jesus gives us through his prayer. This is His calling to each of us as individual disciples. We cannot put it aside and discard this part of Jesus' teaching as something beyond us, something too high for us to reach. Actually, if we are tempted to think along this line we are actually stating truth. Because the truth is, *we* cannot attain to this high standard of discipleship by ourselves. This is why Jesus prayed this prayer for us. It is to be encouraged and strengthened by His prayer so that we will trust Him to make it a reality in our lives and experience. Once again it comes back to faith in Jesus and His Word.

As impossible as it may seem to us as we look at the Church worldwide with its many denominational divisions, if we exercise the kind of faith that Jesus is looking for, I believe we can see amazing things happen for the glory of God—through the people of God. Although the fulfillment of the prayer of Jesus that we **"may be one"** visibly in the eyes of the world may seem unrealistic from a natural viewpoint, from a spiritual viewpoint fortified by the prayers of faith, I believe we can at least see victories in many assemblies of believers who have caught Jesus' vision for unity. For example, this concern for unity in the body of Christ was demonstrated by evangelical Christians who met together to encourage unity and evangelism worldwide. Dr. Bruce Shelley, long-time professor of church history and historical theology at Denver Seminary, reports:

"The 1974 International Congress on World Evangelization, meeting in Lausanne, Switzerland, gave clear evidence of a new maturity in evangelical views of Christian unity. An international group of 142 evangelical leaders under the honorary chairmanship of Billy Graham invited 2,700 participants to the Swiss city to stimulate regional groups for evangelization and then forge the Lausanne Covenant, signed by the vast majority of the participants,

"The Covenant affirms 'that the church's visible unity in truth is God's purpose.' Two reasons support this evangelical stress on oneness: the first is theological, the second pragmatic. The unity of the church, says the Covenant, is a gift of God through the Spirit, made possible by the cross of Christ. 'He is our peace' (Eph. 4:13).

"The pragmatic reason for 'visible unity in the truth' is the 'evangelism…summons us to unity.' How can we preach a gospel of reconciliation and remain unreconciled?' " (Bruce Shelley, *Church History in Plain Language,* Word Publishing, Dallas, Texas. 1995 449).

In view of the above we can see that there have been, and are, various efforts by Christians to accomplish expressions of unity as an effective witness to the unsaved world around us. Jesus prayed for this passionately. The last part of our chapter verse tells us that Jesus wanted His disciples and the world to know with certainty that the Father loved them, **"...that the world may know that You [the Father] sent Me, and have loved them as You have loved Me."** So, He relates the love of the Father for His disciples as another way the world will become aware of the fact that He was **"sent"** by the Father. Yes, we should be glad to testify of our experience of the Father's gracious love for us. It is to be an ongoing reciprocal interaction of intimate fellowship between us and the Father through our mediator and High Priest Jesus Christ.

In all the talk and expressions of the need for unity among God's people the concept and experiential reality in practice of true biblical love is vital. Biblical love could be described in many ways. One way would be to say that the quality of true love in a person should be seen as outgoing to others. It is true that the second great commandment says, **"You shall love your neighbor as yourself,"** and when we think about this, we can see that it places the level of love at the highest of standards. Love for ourselves is part of our natural instinct to take care of our personal needs, but we are challenged by the second commandment to love others with the same care and concern.

Working at the Creation Experience Museum in Branson, Missouri, gives our trained tour guides exposure to thousands of guests with many different church backgrounds and theological beliefs. In general, we find our guests approve of our emphasis on the biblical Creator and the need to know Him in a saving relationship through faith in Jesus Christ. But sometimes we have guests who want to vocally influence others with their particular church or group teachings which can be detrimental to harmony among other members of the tour group. Our tour guides are trained to avoid issues that are controversial theologically, and in a spirit of love tell our guests that we have to keep moving through the museum out of respect for everyone's time. Yes, we sometimes have interesting and sadly controversial guests who, for example, want to influence us and everybody else to believe in a *flat Earth*—no, I'm not joking.

How should we respond to others we come across who espouse teachings that to us seem unnecessary, controversial, not edifying, and maybe even ridiculous? In a nutshell, we must love them, pray for them, and have patience with them like the individual I mentioned previously who said: "I'm out of here." This was when he realized our museum was biblically based *before* he took the tour. However, what he did not know was that in situations like this (not very often so far), after he left, we had a time of prayer for him. Everyone who enters our museum will be prayed for one way or another.

People are very different, even though we are created in the image of God. Just look at the original disciples chosen by Jesus. To get them to love one another as a group was a huge challenge few would have been willing to undertake with relish. So, when Jesus emphasizes the scripture, **"You shall love your neighbor as yourself,"** this is surely one of the greatest challenges we face on Earth when interacting with others. Here is one of several examples we could cite from Scripture and the difficulty experienced by members of the early Church to keep unity and harmony. Philippians 4:2 says, **"I implore Euodia and I implore Syntyche to be of the same mind in the Lord."**

Homer A. Kent, Jr. writes:

"Two women, Euodia and Syntyche, are instructed to bring their attitudes into harmony. Paul does not indicate which one was in the wrong but knows that if the attitude of each would be formed 'in the Lord,' the disharmony would vanish. Repetition of 'I plead' [implore, NKJV] may indicate the need for separate admonitions because the rift between them had become so great. Paul's method of handling the problem suggests that it was not a doctrinal issue, but a clash of personalities." (Barker & Kohlenberger, *The Expositor's Bible Commentary: New Testament.* Zondervan, Grand Rapids. 1994 808).

Here were two individuals who had great difficulty getting along with one another in loving harmony. There is the old saying: Familiarity breeds contempt.

Unfortunately, it can be true even in the marriage relationship—in fact, sadly, very predominant among Christians, as evident through the national plague of divorce. Psychologists have observed that by about the fifth year of marriage a couple may have discovered things about their partners which were not observed before getting married. What is the answer for Christian couples? For each one, first, concentrating less on the perceived faults of your partner, and praying that as an individual your own relationship with the Lord is what it is supposed to be. This is where it should begin. Not with the faults of others, but self-examination before the Lord to learn how to cast the more-than-likely beam out of your own eye before trying to correct the faults of the other person. In other words, if we concentrate first on being who *we* should be in our relationship with God, then by faith we will surely expect God's favor and help for the healing of the relationship in question.

Paul wrote of these two ladies who lacked loving relationships that it would be possible for them to be of **"...the same mind in the Lord."** This is the secret: if as individuals we are truly **"in the Lord"** we will be in the right position to receive the wisdom and direction from the Lord that we need. This is also how we can see unity in the body of Christ as a whole. It takes individuals, one by one, to make sure they are *in the Lord* in their personal relationship with Him. So, we are back once again to the desperate need for personal time to be spent in intimate fellowship with the Lord in prayer and meditation of the Word. Well, am I doing it? Are you doing it?

Chapter 17
The Glorious Future
John 17:24

"Father, I desire that they also whom You gave Me may be with Me where I am, that they may behold My glory which You have given Me; for You loved Me before the foundation of the world."

Our Creator has revealed His desire for His creation from the very beginning. God, in the form He chose to reveal Himself (theophany), spent time with Adam and Eve each day. As extremely intelligent individuals, I personally believe they must have asked God questions about their existence, and I'm sure He answered them. He spoke to them one-on-one and gave them instructions on how to enjoy and look after the beautiful Garden of Eden environment He had created for them. We also get a clue from Genesis 3:8, which says:

"And they heard the sound of the Lord God walking in the garden in the cool of the day, and Adam and his wife hid themselves from the presence of the Lord among the trees of the garden."

However, we know the sad story, and because Adam and Eve failed the test God gave them by disobeying Him, they lost the privilege of being in God's presence. Yet, God created us for the specific purpose of having uninterrupted, intimate fellowship with us. God wants to share Himself with us. Can you imagine anything more glorious than this? For us to have individual, personal relationship with the Creator of all life and all things is a privilege beyond words to describe. Jesus revealed His will and the will of the Father when talking to the disciples with these words:

"Let not your heart be troubled; you believe in God, believe also in Me. In My Father's house are many mansions [dwelling places]; **if it were not so, I would have told you. I go to prepare a place for you. And if I go and prepare a place for you, I will come again and receive you to Myself; that where I am,** *there* **you may be also"** (John 14:1-3).

As mentioned earlier, we believe that Jesus, revealed Himself in a special way to Adam and Eve when He spent time with them in the garden. But sin intervened in history, and our perfectly righteous God had to separate Himself from intimate fellowship with His creation. But now we find Jesus telling His disciples about a wonderful restoration in the future. Once again it will be possible for us to have a personal intimate relationship with our Creator. But this future relationship, He says, will be much superior in quality of experience than that which Adam and Eve enjoyed. Even the place He is preparing for us must be beyond anything we could imagine for its glory and beauty. Jesus said, **"And If I go and prepare a place for you, I will come again and receive you to Myself; that where I am,** *there* **you may be also"** (John 14:3).

Many of the things Jesus taught and revealed to the disciples before the crucifixion were not understood by them. Jesus talked about *going* and *coming back.* And then there are the mysterious words which the disciples began to understand only after the resurrection and the Day of Pentecost. For example, Jesus said, **"I will not leave you orphans** (Greek— *orphanous,* they would not be deserted)**, I will come to you"** (John 14:18). Emotionally, the disciples must certainly have felt like orphans during the time between the crucifixion and the resurrection. In fact, they were totally devastated. They saw their hopes for the future completely dashed and obliterated.

Jesus told the disciples something which they would remember later because He had taught them about a **"Helper"** who would be with them to guide, comfort, and help them. He said:

"And I will pray the Father, and He will give you another Helper (Greek—*parakletos*, advocate and Helper)**, that He may abide with you forever—the Spirit of truth, whom the world cannot receive, because it neither sees Him nor knows Him, for He dwells with you and will be in you"** (John 14:16,17).

Jesus referred to this **"Spirit of truth"** who was *with* the disciples at the time He was speaking to them—with them because of Jesus' presence with them, but then added He **"will be in you."** This was something totally new for the disciples to hear from Jesus, and I don't think they could have even begun to understand the implications of what this would mean for them in the future. How many could have in their wildest dreams ever envisioned a scenario such as what they experienced on the Day of Pentecost? Although they were expecting something to happen while they were waiting in obedience to the command of Jesus which He had given them before ascending to heaven, the events that happened on the Day of Pentecost must have been an absolutely awesome and a complete surprise. They never dreamed they would be speaking the **"wonderful works of God"** (Acts 2:11) perfectly in languages they had never learned.

Only as time passed would the disciples have begun to realize what had happened. For the first time in their experience the presence of God actually resided *within them*. The Bible says, **"And they were all filled with the Holy Spirit"** (Acts 2:4). The same Spirit who was present at the beginning of creation **"...was hovering over the face of the waters"** (Genesis 1:2), had now entered their spirit/soul beings, and was creating within them the ability to minister for the kingdom of God just what Jesus had promised them. In John 14:12-14 we read:

"Most assuredly, I say to you, he who believes in Me, the works that I do he will do also; and greater *works* than these he will do because I go to My Father. And whatever you ask in My name, that I will do, that the Father may be glorified in the Son. If you ask anything in My name, I will do *it*."

This is the glorious gift our Lord has given and made available for all who believe in Him. Just as Jesus said, this is a privilege that is only for those with a believing relationship with Him: **"he who believes."** Those of the unsaved world do not understand and **"...cannot receive, because it** [the unsaved world] **neither sees Him nor knows Him** [the Holy Spirit]**"** (John 14:17). This is why we would say that true Christianity must be experiential as well as intellectual. Theological knowledge about God by itself is completely different from having the living presence of God the Holy Spirit living within one's spirit/soul being. The English reformer and preacher John Wesley was discouraged with all his religious activities, until one day his heart was "strangely warmed" as he came into a new experience of God's grace and salvation with the aid of the Holy Spirit. His experience is described:

"John Wesley was almost in despair. He did not have the faith to continue to preach. When death stared him in the face, he was fearful and found little comfort in his religion. To Peter Böhler, a Moravian friend, he confessed his growing misery and decision to give up the ministry. Böhler counseled otherwise. "Preach faith till you have it," he advised. "And then because you have it, you will preach faith." ...John acted on the advice. He led a prisoner to Christ by preaching faith in Christ alone for forgiveness of sins. The prisoner was immediately converted. John was astonished...he reluctantly attended a meeting in Aldersgate. Someone read from Luther's Preface to the Epistle to Romans. About 8:45 p.m. "while he was describing the change which God works in the heart through faith in Christ, I felt my heart strangely warmed. I felt I did trust in Christ, Christ alone for salvation; and an assurance was given me that He had taken away my sins, even mine, and [had thus] saved me from the law of sin and death." (https://www.christianity.com/church/churchhistory/timeline/1701-1800/john-wesleys-heart-strangely-warmed-11630227.html. Accessed 11-28-20).

Was this new experience that happened to the disciples on the Day of Pentecost more meaningful to them than their previous actual physical relationship with Jesus during the three years of His ministry? I would think that it would have to be so. Having the knowledge and experience of God's presence actually living within and continually filling one (as dependent on a continual intimate relationship with Him) with power, love, joy and peace beyond anything the world could offer, is definitely something absolutely incomparable. However, we know these original disciples could never forget those physical years with Jesus. John writes: **"That which was from the beginning, which we have heard, which we have seen with our eyes, and our hands have handled, concerning the Word of life"** (1 John 1:1).

This is why our Lord desires such intimate fellowship with us, so that not only will we enjoy such closeness, but that we will be His willing servants in the work of the kingdom of God. We need His strength to do the even **"greater things"** (John 14:12) than He did, and if we *believe without doubting* or mental reservation, we will truly see God be fruitful through our lives for His glory.

Jesus prayed that **"they may behold My glory."** So, I believe we could look at this prayer of Jesus as pertaining to both present experiences as well as for the future. How do we see His glory today? Notice that it is the glory of Jesus, **"My glory,"** that Jesus prayed His disciples would recognize. How were they going to see Christ's glory when He had ascended into heaven and they could not see Him visibly anymore? I imagine that the disciples could envision Christ's glorious reign in the future consummation of things as they began to understand more of God's purposes, but how were they to see Christ's glory in the here and now? Before I attempt to answer this question from the New Testament perspective, there are some interesting references to *glory* in the Old Testament that would be good to examine.

During the wilderness travels of the children of Israel, the older generation found themselves in the undesirable, harsh desert environment because they had not believed God to give them victory over the giants inhabiting the land of Canaan. Could we learn a lesson from this, that when Christians don't believe God for victory when faced with the strength and opposition of the enemy, the Church may go through a desert-like experience where the Gospel is not advancing? It will not be God's fault! It is easy to make complaints about our situation, but if we know that God is with us we should trust Him to see us through each and every trial. James writes: **"My brethren, count it all joy when you fall into various trials"** (James 1:2). Although this would not be the natural human reaction to difficulties, guess what will happen if we do this sincerely, God *will* see us through. Only Joshua and Caleb, of the twelve spies, believed in God's strength to help them, and they were the only two people of that generation who actually entered the Promised Land forty years later.

Many times the children of Israel complained about the difficulties they were facing during those wilderness travels. But in spite of this, God supplied their needs and even gave them physical evidence of His presence with them. For example, when they were complaining to God about their desire for more food such as they had been used to in Egypt, we read:

"Then the Lord said to Moses, 'Behold, I will rain bread from heaven for you. And the people shall go out and gather a certain quota every day, that I may test them, whether they will walk in My law or not...And in the morning you shall see the glory of the Lord...they looked toward the wilderness, and behold, the glory of the Lord appeared in the cloud' " (Exodus 16:4,7,10).

The Lord demonstrated His majestic creative power by supplying bread and meat for the people. The bread was known as *manna* and continued for the entire 40 years of the wilderness wanderings. Also, the Lord supplied water for the people miraculously when Moses was instructed to strike a rock (Exodus 17:6).

Again, we could take valuable spiritual lessons from these historical events, because as Christians in this twenty-first century we should certainly trust in the Lord for our supply of *spiritual* food and drink. And, since as Christians we must all partake of the same spiritual nutrition, such knowledge should help to keep us humble enough to accept our brothers and sisters with a unity we should all be experiencing in Him. Putting something supernatural into simple language, Jesus is our food and drink—our living Word and drink through the Spirit. Just as it takes time to partake of physical food and drink, so we should make sure we do the same for the more important spiritual sustenance we can enjoy as we live in close fellowship with the Father, our High Priest Jesus, and the Holy Spirit. Although it was difficult at the time for those who heard the words of Jesus to grasp His meaning, He nevertheless said:

"I am the bread of life. Your fathers ate the manna in the wilderness, and are dead. This is the bread which comes down from heaven, that one may eat of it and not die...Most assuredly I say to you, unless you eat the flesh of the Son of Man and drink His blood, you have no life in you. Whoever eats My flesh and drinks My blood has eternal life, and I will raise him up at the last day" (John 6:48-50,53,54).

The miraculous supply of food and drink for the children of Israel in the wilderness was certainly tangible evidence of God's real presence and care for them, but a greater manifestation of His glory and power was soon to come. When the people arrived at Mt. Sinai we read:

"Moses went up to God, and the Lord called to him from the mountain" (Exodus 19:3). **"And the Lord said to Moses, 'Behold, I come to you in the thick cloud, that the people may hear when I speak with you, and believe you forever...For on the third day the Lord will come down upon Mount Sinai in the sight of all the people"** (Exodus 19:9,11).

It must have been an awesome sight and experience for the people of Israel to see this unique manifestation of a mountain that literally burned with supernatural fire. The record says:

"Then it came to pass on the third day, in the morning, that there were thunderings and lightenings, and a thick cloud on the mountain; and the sound of the trumpet was very loud, so that all the people who *were* in the camp trembled...Now Mount Sinai *was* completely in smoke, because the Lord descended upon it in fire" (Exodus 19:16,18).

Certainly this was a demonstration of God's glory to the people, but at that time under what has been called the dispensation of law, it was an evidence of a holy God to whom the average people were not allowed close relationship or proximity. But Moses, who had the incredible privilege of personal face-to-face (Exodus 33:11, but not seeing a physical face) communication and intimacy with God, also had the desire for even more revelation of God's glory. He expressed his desire with this prayer:

"Now therefore, I pray, if I have found grace in Your sight, show me now Your way, that I may know you and that I may find grace in Your sight…And He said, 'My Presence will go *with you*, and I will give you rest" (Exodus 33:13,14).

Moses also prayed, **"Please, show me Your glory"** (Exodus 33:18).

God replied:

"I will make all My goodness pass before you, and I will proclaim the name of the Lord before you…You cannot see My face; for no man shall see Me, and live…So it shall be, while My glory passes by, that I will put you in the cleft of the rock, and will cover you with My hand while I pass by. Then I will take away My hand, and you shall see My back; but My face shall not be seen" (Exodus 33:19,20,22,23).

What an amazing otherworldly supernatural experience this was for Moses. When he came down from the mountain the people were afraid of him. He did not realize that because of the time he had been in God's presence it had caused his face to shine supernaturally. So, how does all of this relate to Christians and unity in the twenty-first century? So back to the question: How do we see the glory of God in the here and now? The answer is simply by the presence of the Holy Spirit working within us and through us. The veil Moses had to wear because of his shining face is symbolic of the

Jewish people today who have not accepted Jesus as their Messiah. But when a Jewish person believes in Jesus as Messiah they begin to see the glory of the Lord by the Holy Spirit. Paul writes about the transition from the Old Testament Jewish revelation of glory to the New Testament Christian experience:

"But their [Jewish] **minds were blinded. For until this day the same veil remains unlifted in the reading of the Old Testament, because the *veil* is taken away in Christ...But even to this day, when Moses is read, a veil lies on their heart. Nevertheless when one turns to the Lord, the veil is taken away. Now the Lord is the Spirit; and where the Spirit of the Lord *is* there is liberty.**

But we all, with unveiled face, beholding as in a mirror the glory of the Lord, are being transformed into the same image from glory to glory, just as by the Spirit of the Lord" (2 Corinthians 3:14-18).

Yes, we behold the glory of the Lord through Holy-Spirit revelation through the means of feeding on His living Word and intimate relationship with Him through prayer. Moses spent a lot of time in the Holy Place of the wilderness tent in conversation with God. How much time do we spend?

We have the glorious privilege of having the very presence of God the Holy Spirit residing in our spirit/soul beings. How incredible that so many who have been deeply involved in sinful lifestyles can be radically transformed into a holy saints of God. It is the miracle of the grace of God. Again, Jesus' desire for His believing saints is, **"that they may behold My glory."** We can catch a glimpse and a little foretaste of His glory here on earth in the lives of His overcoming saints, especially if we are corporately one with Him in unity. However, when the time comes we are actually with Him in the place He is preparing for us in the heavenly realm known as **"In My Father's house"** (John 14:2), it will be a revelation beyond description. Am I, and are you, revealing the glory of the Lord through your life today?

Chapter 18
Experiencing His Love
John 17:25,26

"O righteous Father! The world has not known You, but I have known You; and these have known that You sent Me. And I have declared to them Your name, and will declare *it*, that the love with which You loved Me may be in them, and I in them."

First John 4:8 says, **"God is love."** We know that God's purpose in creating our world in the first place was because He wanted a people who would willingly, of their own free will and independent choice, wholeheartedly love Him and be in fellowship with Him. How does God, being the personal God that He is, feel about the multitudes of Earth's population today who have not responded to His love? God does express personal emotional feelings. At the tomb of Lazarus it says, **"Jesus wept"** (John 11:35). Of course, we know that there are many in the world who have never had the opportunity to hear of a God of love, but the comforting truth is to know that because God is a God of love, He is also the perfect Judge of all peoples. All people have the inherent moral knowledge of right and wrong which God has implanted in them.

In the chapter verse above Jesus starts by referring to the Father as **"righteous."** Among other things, a righteous God would be one of complete impartiality with His creation. His love would be extended to all. Because of His perfect righteousness He would treat everyone with absolute fairness. All would be treated equally. But men often fail to follow the pathway of love offered to them through the gospel, or worse, distort its true message. James writes about the need for believers to emulate godly qualities of love and respect when interacting among our earthly acquaintances—especially our Christian brothers and sisters. He writes:

"My brethren do not hold the faith of our Lord Jesus Christ, *the Lord* of glory, with partiality. For if there should come into your assembly a man with gold rings, in fine apparel, and there should also come in a poor man in filthy clothes, and you pay attention to the one wearing the fine clothes and say to him, 'You sit here in a good place,' and say to the poor man, 'You stand there,' or, 'Sit here at my footstool,' have you not shown partiality among yourselves, and become judges with evil thoughts?" (James 2:1-4).

The incident James portrays is an example of the fact that people can very easily fall into the worldly, uncaring attitude of self-importance, condescension and selfishness. In other words, adult humans can be just like newborn infants who very quickly make known their perception of life that "it's all about me"—and they usually do so quite loudly! People talk about climbing the ladder of success, but unfortunately, so many times it means trampling over others, pushing them down and out of the way in order to get to the top by all means possible. Of course, this kind of philosophy is encouraged by God's enemy, Satan, whose work is to cause disorder, disruption, hatred, and as much anti-God activity as possible. So, just as the Apostle John reminds us that, **"...even now many antichrists have come"** (1 John 2:18), we see the opposite of what God wants. He desires love and unity, but the world, the flesh, and the devil combined are out to deceive and destroy any semblance of a God who cares and loves.

As a Christian, I have to be glad that my God is perfectly righteous. Guilty as a sinner and still making mistakes today, I am so thankful that God did not let me in any way think that I was going to be accepted by

Him unless I came the way He has provided—through Jesus Christ. But as a believer who has trusted in Christ alone, and His atoning sacrifice through the shedding of His blood, it is something wonderful, yet beyond my full comprehension, to know that I am **"accepted in the Beloved"** (Ephesians 1:6).

Yes, I experience His love and fellowship through my personal relationship with Him. Experiencing His love is, of course, something that all true believers should know for themselves. And if there is a flow of God's love through individual believers there should surely be an extension of the same through the corporate body of Christ. Here is the amazing request of Jesus for those who follow Him: *He wants us to love one another with the same degree of love the Father bestows on Him.* This surely seems like a high and lofty goal, but Jesus prayed for it. Read it again from our chapter verse:

"...that the love with which You [the Father] **loved Me may be in them."**

How extensive is the love of the Father for the Son? Surely, if the body of Christ had even a small portion of such incomprehensible love it would solve all our lack of unity and denominational divisions. Since Jesus prayed that this level of divine love **"be in them,"** I feel the need to exercise some self-examination to try to find out where I stand before the Lord in this matter of supreme importance. Is there anything in my life that is hindering God's will in this matter? Then the question for me would be: How extensive is *my love* for the Father and the Son?

Are there degrees of love? On the natural human level, we can see outward evidence for different degrees of emotional love. For example, we could say that the love of a mother for her child will naturally be of a stronger degree than her love for a friend or neighbor. And then we all tend to have our favorite Christian friends with whom we enjoy fellowship in rather closed, independent circles. Jesus revealed through His prayer that it is possible for us to have such a high degree of love that it will have the effect of producing Christlikeness within us. To be like Jesus is, of course, the ultimate goal for us as followers of Christ. A powerful message is given to us on love through the interaction between Jesus and the Apostle Peter in the following scripture:

"Jesus said to Simon Peter, 'Simon, *son* of Jonah, do you love [Greek—*agapas*] **Me more than these?' He said to Him, 'Yes, Lord; You know that I love** [Greek—*philo*] **You.' He said to him, 'Feed My lambs.' "**

"He said to him again a second time, 'Simon, *son* of Jonah, do you love [Greek—*agapas*] **Me?' He said to Him, 'Yes, Lord; You know that I love** [Greek—*philo*] **You.' He said to him, 'Tend My sheep.' "**

"He said to him the third time, 'Simon, *son* of Jonah, do you love [Greek—*phileis*] **Me?' Peter was grieved because He said to him the third time, 'Do you love** [Greek—*phileis*] **Me?' And he said to Him, 'Lord, You know all things; You know that I love** [Greek—*philo*] **You.' Jesus said to him, 'Feed My sheep' "** (John 21:15-17).

Many of us have probably heard messages preached on this passage with explanation given to the meaning of the different Greek words used by Jesus and Peter for the word *love*. Simply put, the Greek word *agapas* is considered to represent a much deeper quality of love than *philo*. In English we could distinguish the meanings by thinking of the difference between a very *close bond of love* such as that between a husband and wife, and that of a lesser kind of love between friends we could liken to the word *affection*. We can see in this scripture that Peter, perhaps because of his embarrassment for denying his relationship with the Lord during Jesus' illegal trial, could not bring himself to use the word *agapas*—the higher degree of love. However, we are well aware of the fact that later Peter laid down his life for the Lord. Tradition tells us he was crucified under the Roman Emperor Nero about A.D. 67, but insisted on being crucified upside down because he did not feel worthy to be crucified in the same way as Jesus. Jesus said:

"He who has My commandments and keeps them, it is he who loves Me. And he who loves Me will be loved by My father, and I will love him and manifest Myself to him" (John 14:21).

Obedience! It is a word we had to learn to live with from a young age—most of us at times reluctantly, I'm sure. We can identify the early independent nature of infants with the sin nature we have all inherited from Adam. We knew we were loved by our parents (except for sad situations where love was absent), and as we grew up and matured, we realized that obedience to good rules and following good advice from our parents and others contributed to harmony and pleasant relationships. In the above verse Jesus says that a test of our love for Him depends on whether or not we are keeping His commandments. Both Jesus and His earthly brother James (transliterated Jacob from the Greek) emphasized the importance of *doing* to show sincerity of purpose. Jesus taught:

"Therefore whoever hears these sayings of Mine, and does them, I will liken him to a wise man who built his house on the rock: and the rain descended, the floods came, and the winds blew and beat on that house; and it did not fall, for it was founded on the rock."

"But everyone who hears these sayings of Mine, and does not do them, will be like a foolish man who built his house on the sand: and the rain descended, the floods came, and the winds blew

and beat on that house; and it fell. And great was its fall" (Matthew 7:24 -27).

So, we have to ask ourselves: Are we *doing* the sayings or commands of Jesus in addition to hearing them? James echoes the words of Jesus in his epistle:

"But be doers of the word, and not hearers only, deceiving yourselves. For if anyone is a hearer of the word and not a doer, he is like a man observing his natural face in a mirror; for he observes himself, goes away, and immediately forgets what kind of man he was...Thus also faith by itself, if it does not have works, is dead" (James 1:22-24; 2:17).

If the pure love of God resides in our hearts there should surely be some outward evidence of it expressed to others around us, unless we live the life of a hermit. There have been periods of history when individuals thought the only way to be sure they could live a holy life was to separate themselves from all social contact with others as much as possible. But, just as the disciples of our Lord while still in His physical presence had to overcome challenges with different personalities among themselves, so we are faced with like situations in our daily lives. Of course, we cannot fail to mention the great challenge that First Corinthians chapter 13 brings to us:

"Though I speak with the tongues of men and of angels, but have not love, I have become sounding brass or a clanging cymbal. And though I have *the gift of* prophecy, and understand all mysteries and all knowledge, and though I have all faith, so that I could remove mountains, but have not love, I am nothing" (1 Corinthians 13:1,2).

How can I be **"nothing?"** By trying to minister to others through the gifts of the Spirit, speaking or praying in tongues, prophesying and exercising great miracles of faith without being motivated by genuine love. The other side of the coin would be that if I do these things with a true heart of ministry, they can be tremendously effective for edifying and advancing the work of the kingdom of God. The passage continues:

"And though I bestow all my goods to feed *the poor*, and though I give my body to be burned, but have not love, it profits me nothing" (1 Corinthians 13:3).

How can I not profit? There have always been altruistic desires within the emotional hearts of good people to engage in social welfare by helping others with the necessities of life. The Salvation Army and many individual churches are careful to do this, which is good as long as the spiritual message is faithfully included. And all of this is obviously acceptable and beneficial to all. But doing so with the underlying motive of earning God's special favor and the favor of others is not guaranteed to profit one eternally. Helping others materially should always be a desire and means of service in which Christians should willingly participate, and Jesus certainly gave His approval of such when a young man of considerable material means asked Him how to attain eternal life. Jesus said:

"If you want to be perfect, go, sell what you have and give to the poor, and you will have treasure in heaven; and come, follow Me." But when the young man heard that saying, he went away sorrowful, for he had great possessions" (Matthew 19:21).

Apparently, this young man had not been in the habit of giving any kind of material help to those around him who were not so blessed. I have often wondered if this young man eventually overcame this hindrance in his life and became a follower of Jesus. The abundance of riches can be the very thing that draws people away from a loving relationship with God and others. Even family members who have appeared to be in close relationship with one another for years can experience great hurt, anger, and lack of harmony when the time comes to divide an inheritance. The Bible, in both the Old and New Testaments, has several things to say to us about the very real danger of material riches and the false sense of security they can bring. Here are just a few:

"For the Lord your God is bringing you into a good land...a land in which you will eat bread without scarcity, in which you will lack nothing...When you have eaten and are full...Beware that you do not forget the Lord your God by not keeping His commandments" (Deuteronomy 8:7,9-11).

"Give me neither poverty nor riches—Feed me with the food allotted to me; lest I be full and deny *You*, and say, 'Who is the Lord?' " (Proverbs 30:8,9).

"No servant can serve two masters; for either he will hate the one and love the other, or else he will be loyal to the one and despise the other. You cannot serve God and mammon [money or wealth]" (Luke 16:13).

"But those who desire to be rich fall into temptation and a snare, and *into* many foolish and harmful lusts which drown men in destruction and perdition. For the love of money is a root of all *kinds of* evil, for which some have strayed from the faith in their greediness, and pierced themselves through with many sorrows" (1 Timothy 6:9,10).

Yes, the accumulation of money and wealth can very easily be an instrument of the enemy to extinguish our love for the Lord. Christians should always be on the alert for anything that could affect their calling and personal relationship with God. This is because each individual member of the body of Christ affects the unity of the rest of the corporate body of believers—positively or negatively. Returning and continuing with the scripture in Corinthians we read:

"Love suffers long *and* is kind; love does not envy; love does not parade itself, is not puffed up [arrogant]; **does not behave rudely, does not seek its own, is not provoked, thinks no evil; does not rejoice in iniquity, but rejoices in the truth; bears all things, believes all things, hopes all things, endures all things. Love never fails"** (1 Corinthians 13:4-8).

Wow! What can love not do? Each phrase in this passage would lend itself to long commentary for expounding its meanings and implications. If **"love never fails"** it should be obvious to all of us as believers that we should be exercising our efforts to be part of the solution for any lack of unity in our fellowships. We need to aim for our personal input to our local fellowship to be edifying with the pure love of God. Let us meditate with prayerful consideration on these scriptures. I believe the Word will speak for itself to each individual heart, so I leave you, the reader, with this simple exhortation: pray, meditate, believe.

Chapter 19
Divisions: A Bumpy Road

"Now I plead with you, brethren, by the name of our Lord Jesus Christ, that you all speak the same thing, and *that* there be no divisions [schisms] among you, but that you be perfectly joined together in the same mind and in the same judgment" (1 Corinthians 1:10).

"Only let your conduct be worthy of the gospel of Christ, so that whether I come and see you or am absent, I may hear of your affairs, that you stand fast in one spirit, with one mind striving together for the faith of the gospel" (Philippians 1:27)

"...fulfill my joy by being likeminded, having the same love, *being* of one accord, of one mind" (Philippians 2:2).

"Now I urge you brethren, note those who cause divisions and offenses, contrary to the doctrine which you learned, and avoid them" (Romans 16:17).

Notice from the verses above that even in the first century the Apostle Paul already had great concern for unity among the Christians to whom he had ministered. There were already serious issues he realized needed to be addressed. He was concerned for them to be of the **"same mind, same judgment, with one mind, one accord."** This indicates that some of these early Christians needed guidance in truth and would have to humbly admit they had been influenced by false teaching. Satan has obviously always found false teaching to be a tremendously effective weapon against God's people to bring disunity and disruption. However, as false teaching is exposed it is never easy for anyone to confess, "I was wrong!" Human pride is often a king difficult to depose!

Finding out that some things you have believed and thought to be true may not be so, can be an unpleasant, humiliating, and unnerving personal experience—especially if you are known as a preacher or teacher of the Word. This is why James wrote:

"My brethren, let not many of you become teachers, knowing that we shall receive a stricter judgment" (James 3:1).

In other words, James is telling us to be aware of the awesome responsibility of communicating the Word of God. Typically, our human nature is not well-disposed to being told we are wrong about anything. I don't even like it when my wife tells me first thing in the morning that I was the one who left the front door unlocked—when I'm sure it was her! Of course, this would be akin to our regular day-to-day experiences we all go through. But dealing with more sensitive issues like doctrinal differences is a very tough field to tackle with the hope of leaving everyone happy with their theological and doctrinal batting order.

After Luther's dramatic rebellion in rejecting certain Catholic teachings and his conviction of *sola biblia* (*by Scripture alone*), there were many variations and different shades of doctrinal beliefs that sprang up, especially in the seventeenth century. In the midst of all of this some were deeply concerned for the spiritual unity of the body of Christ. One of these was Philipp J. Spener who was concerned about the drift to formalism in emerging Protestantism. In 1675 he wrote a book titled *Pia Desideria* (*"The Piety We Desire"* or *"Heartfelt Desire for God-pleasing Reform"*), listing six goals for application to the Christian life:

1. Intensified study of the Bible.
2. Fuller exercise by the laity of their spiritual priesthood.

3. Emphasis on the heart and not the head in matters of faith.
4. Charity in doctrinal controversies which should be directed toward winning hearts and not in proving who is right.
5. Reorganizing of theological studies in seminaries.
6. Revival or preaching as a proclamation of the personal truths embedded in the gospel.

(*Nelson's New Christian Dictionary,* Thomas Nelson, 2001 608).

This was Spener's attempt to emphasize what he believed to be the greatest need for inner devotion of the heart in real spiritual experience. Such influence of pietism can also be seen through the English reformer John Wesley and other holiness movements. The main concern, as mentioned, was again that the divisions dividing the body of Christ should be smoothed out somehow so there would be an uncompromised witness to the world of the unity and true brotherhood of Christian love. This was the concern of many Christians during that period of the seventeenth century. But unfortunately, the doctrinal differences expressed have not resulted in more unity, but a continuation of division because of these distinctive beliefs, even though some differences could be looked upon as rather minor, theologically.

We, the body of Christ, are supposed to be a team working together harmoniously for the good of the whole. Not only *supposed to be,* but in reality commanded to be by our Lord as we have seen in the previous chapters. This is why I feel strongly about differences in doctrine that are not only seen by the secular world looking on as a bad testimony for Christianity in general, but because the disparities between us as believers are contrary to the very heart's desire of our Savior. Therefore, I have a noteworthy aphorism which I believe expresses my passion about this subject and the reason for writing this book:

I am deeply concerned about anything that causes unnecessary division in the body of Christ.

Unnecessary division! It was happening in Corinth and other early churches two thousand years ago, and it is still with us in the first quarter of our own twenty-first century. If I don't have the same spiritual and passionate concern about this issue as Paul demonstrated—and surely His concern was influenced by the Holy Spirit—then there must be a lack in my understanding of how important this matter is to our Lord. The prayer of Jesus we looked at in the previous chapters makes it as clear as it could possibly be that our Creator God, who is a God of love, intends to have a people for all eternity who love each other as He loves—i.e., with the supreme and special quality of pure, holy, godly love.

After prayer I have decided not to go into the actual details of the doctrinal differences we observe in the body of Christ as originally intended. It is obvious that our very active enemy has been able to promote disunity—especially within the Protestant expressions of faith, as well as some of the well-known different doctrinal distinctives between historic Catholic and Protestant beliefs. Satan has managed to generate theological potholes for professed believers to fall into, and uses them as wedges to divide God's people. Unfortunately, he has obviously had tremendous success.

I want my readers to know that in no way am I setting myself up as a judge of people or their beliefs, for I would not dare to presume such a course before the Lord. That is God's realm alone. But I believe I have the right scripturally (as does any Christian) to put to the test beliefs that may be totally unorthodox from basic evangelical biblical Christian doctrine. There is something the Apostle Paul felt led to write as a principle for practical implementation that should involve all of us—especially mature Christians. It has to do with our response to hearing the Word of God preached or taught, and very importantly concerns the edification of the body of Christ with truth. In 1 Corinthians 14:29 Paul writes: **"Let the prophets speak two or three, and let the others judge."** The word **"judge"** from the Greek *diakrinetosan* is from the root *diakrino*. W. E. Vine explains:

> "Signifies 'to separate, discriminate'; then, 'to learn by discriminating, to determine, decide.' And in 1 Corinthians 11:29, with reference to partaking of the bread and the cup of the Lord's Supper unworthily, by not 'discerning' one's condition,;...regarding oral testimony in a gathering of believers, it is used of 'discerning' what is of the Holy Spirit" (W. E. Vine, *An Expository Dictionary of New Testament Words*. Fleming H. Revell Company, New Jersey, 1966 315).

Therefore, the understanding of what Paul was saying here indicates that when someone is engaged in public speaking, teaching, preaching, or even what we could call prophetic proclamation, the other believers listening should accept responsibility for discerning, evaluating and weighing carefully what is being said. This is not to judge the person, but to evaluate and discern the truth and value of what is being ministered for the benefit of the whole assembly.

How are we supposed to do this? The short answer is by comparison with the revealed will of God in the Word of God. But of course, although this must always be the first answer, there is more to it than this—in fact; we should remember that these early Christians did not have the whole Bible as we do today. So, Paul would have surely expected those doing the discerning to be of sufficient maturity and knowledge in the truth of God's Word (with whatever scrolls and manuscripts were available to them at that time) and their own personal relationship with the Lord. He would, for example, expect the listening Christians to be filled with the Holy Spirit and be able to sense the validity or not of what was being said with the help of the same Holy Spirit. Jesus said, **"When He, the Spirit of truth, has come, He will guide you into all truth"** (John 16:13).

Scripturally speaking, Christians are not expected to sit and listen to someone expounding the Gospel and the Word of God without seriously considering whether what they are hearing is the truth or not. One may often hear things that seem questionable, or more seriously, that are obviously scripturally wrong. But unfortunately, it seems that the majority of believers do not personally engage in actively checking and comparing what they hear with the Word of God.

One of the reasons for this and I will be blunt, is that they don't know their Bibles well enough to participate in such evaluation. Jesus made a statement I believe to be extremely significant related to this subject. He said, **"Take heed what you hear"** (Mark 4:24). In other words, be careful what you listen to and to what you are exposed. Don't just accept everything you hear without checking it out. We should be diligent to exercise the minds given to us by God for such an important exercise as this. Could laziness be a factor? How many of us would want to passively and knowingly sit under teaching we doubt to be completely in line with the truth of the Bible?

Why did the Apostle Paul have to **"plead"** (exhort, appeal) with the Christians at Corinth not to have **"divisions"** or schisms among themselves? Because in truth, they *did* have divisions! We sometimes use the phrase, "I guess it's just human nature" to explain and excuse the habits, failures, weaknesses or personality quirks of another. Well, there is truth in this expression because there is something within us that we were all born with, and that is the sinful nature received from Adam's DNA. And this sinful human nature, without the influence of the fruit of the Holy Spirit, can be quite ugly. This is why Paul needed to write, **"...bearing with one another in love"** (Ephesians 4:2). Unfortunately, history contains a record of some of the most horrific acts perpetrated by those bearing the name of Christian against others bearing that same name.

But true followers of Christ are supposed to be different. If we are where we should be in our relationship with the Lord—that is, humble, seeking the Lord daily through prayer and meditation in the Word— we should be the easiest of all people to get along with. What is the foundational key for generating harmony among God's people? It is divine love in our hearts, flowing out from us to others as emphasized previously in the above chapters. And even though we may be pleasant in company with others, we must still always be bold enough to practice **"... speaking the truth in love"** (Ephesians 4:15). We sometimes tell visitors to our museum that we are in a sense radical, because we declare: Why not accept the message and teaching of the Bible just the way God has given it to us?

I can almost hear someone thinking: It is a lot more complicated than that. Yes, I know there are passages in the Bible that still leave commentators wondering what the real meaning is, and in several situations, we certainly do need extra insight and revelation from the Holy Spirit. The Bible is what it is. We do not have the right to add to it, subtract from it, or change it in any other way. So, I believe the best approach is the simple one (theological buffs will probably not be excited by this stance). In view of this commitment to the simple approach the Bible says:

"But I fear, lest somehow, as the serpent deceived Eve by his craftiness, so your minds may be corrupted from the simplicity that is in Christ" (2 Corinthians 11:3).

Some people just don't feel comfortable with things being simple and straight forward. But God did not provide the Holy-Spirit inspired Scriptures to be understood *only* by those who complicate the truth with their esoteric deep theology. One does not need a degree in higher education to know and understand the way of salvation.

Following is a very general list representing different streams of beliefs that cause divisions among professed Christians:

1. Catholic/Protestant
2. Luther/Zwingli/Calvin/Arminius
3. Sabbath/Sunday
4. Spiritual gifts/Cessationism
5. KJV/Translations
6. Holiness/Apostolic/Orthodox
7. Hyper grace/Orthodox
8. Universalism/Orthodox
9. Liberal/Conservative
10. Creationism/Theistic Evolution
11. Anabaptist/Amish/Mennonite/Orthodox
12. Mormon/Jehovah's Witness/Orthodox

As I have written above, after prayer I have decided not to discuss in detail the theological differences of the representative groups just listed. There is already a plethora of books available for people to study these theological issues. I cannot change anyone's beliefs. Only the Holy Spirit combined with a willing acceptance of the Word of God can even begin to do such a thing. In fact, Scripture gives us a powerful reminder of the problem the Lord Himself had with believers that was not too many years after the resurrection. Consider the following:

I wonder how the first-century Christians in the Church at Ephesus may have reacted to these words of Jesus:

"Nevertheless, I have *this* against you..." Or, to the Church at Pergamos: **"But I have a few things against you."** Or, to the Christians at Thyatira: **"Nevertheless, I have a few things against you."** Or, to the Church at Sardis: **"You have a name that you are alive, but you are dead."** Or, to the Church at Laodicea: **"Because you are lukewarm, and neither cold nor hot, I will vomit you out of My mouth"** (Revelation 2:4,14,20; 3:1,16).

If we are so independent and proud (God hates pride) to think that others may need doctrinal correction but not ourselves, we should immediately run for our prayer closets and listen to the Lord very carefully. The Bible makes clear our need to submit to Scripture as the guide for our beliefs. We should all be concerned that the Scriptures are held and revered as the highest authority. Again, the Bible is what it is, and we should all humble ourselves to let the truth fall where it should—even if it hurts.

"All Scripture is given by inspiration of God, and *is* profitable for doctrine, for reproof, for correction, for instruction in righteousness, that the man of God may be complete, thoroughly equipped for every good work" (2 Timothy 3:16,17).

Obedience to the Scriptures is something that all professing Christians should be totally committed to, every moment of their daily lives. The well-known scripture above gives us the foundation from which to examine our beliefs and come to the understanding of whether they are in line with the truth or not. The Word of God is truth. Jesus, the living Word, is truth. With such a God-given resource as the inspired Scriptures, not to mention the promise and gracious help through the indwelling of the Holy Spirit, one would think there would be very little disagreement about doctrinal beliefs. Surely with all this help we should be experiencing great harmony and oneness in faith with other members of the body of Christ.

Yet, we experience the same problem of divisions and schisms in the Church that the Apostle Paul was faced with in those early days of Christianity. What is the basis of the problem? If we can find out how professing Christians have been led into so many different directions in their understanding of the Scriptures, perhaps we can see more clearly the way ahead to remedy the situation. My involvement in the biblical creation museum ministry brings me into contact with many people who come from a large variety of church backgrounds. One way we try to help people enlarge their vision of truth is to tell them that this ministry is nondenominational and that, as I wrote above, we say: Why not accept the message and teaching of the Bible just the way God has given it to us?

Every professed Christian should be familiar with the warnings given in the Bible concerning adding or subtracting from Scripture. Proverbs 30:6 says: **"Do not add to His words, lest He rebuke you, and you be found a liar."** And a very serious warning given in Revelation 22:18,19 which reads:

"For I testify to everyone who hears the words of the prophecy of this book: If anyone adds to these things, God will add to him the plagues that are written in this book; and if anyone takes away from the word of the book of this prophecy, God shall take away his part from the Book of Life, from the holy city, and *from* the things which are written in this book."

So, divisions are with us. Humanly speaking, it would seem impossible to bring all the varying doctrinal beliefs into a unity of the faith. Yet, the challenge and command of Jesus to His Church is that we should all be moving in the direction of acceptance of our brethren who see some things differently from us. Just like the beginnings of a revival or spiritual renewal, such moving toward unity among believers will need to begin with individuals. There will be obstacles of personal prejudice to overcome, but with the help of the Holy Spirit we could see miracles of unity develop among believers that will begin to fulfill the prayer of Jesus, **"...that they all may be one, as You, Father, *are* in Me, and I in You; that they also may be one in Us, that the world may believe that You sent Me"** (John 17:21).

Let us pray for the bumpy road to become smooth.

Chapter 20
The Answer: Prayer and Fasting
"In fastings often..."
(2 Corinthians 11:27).

Let's not try to make it mean less than what the Bible plainly indicates about the Christian discipline of fasting. True fasting is not turning off the TV for a week. Fasting fundamentally means not putting solid food into your stomach for a chosen period of time. Why would the Apostle Paul share this part of his life with us? Could this have anything to do with his amazing success in spreading the gospel over wide geographical areas during his life—in spite of severe physical persecution? I personally believe this to be absolutely true! Yet, as we now realize, this subject of fasting has not been emphasized greatly in the centuries since Paul, and to this day is somewhat rare for one to hear much about it in many of today's churches, as something of importance for Christians. In fact, many Christians may think of fasting as something monks did in monasteries in the Middle Ages that is of no consequence or importance for believers today.

One would think it would be enough to convince sincere Christians of the importance of incorporating fasting into their lives, since our Lord Jesus Himself practiced it and taught it. In fact, it is obvious from His teaching that He expected His followers to practice fasting as part of their lives and service to Him. This will probably come as a surprise to most Christians. But it has been pointed out by others that Jesus did not teach **"If"** but **"When"** related to a believer's three observances of giving, praying, and fasting. He said:

"Therefore, *when* you do a charitable deed...And *when* you pray...Moreover, *when* you fast..." (Matthew 6:2,5,16, emphasis mine).

So, does God want to punish us in order to keep us humble during our earthly sojourn? Going without food can certainly be uncomfortable for both our physical and mental sensitivities, but there is a secret that only those who have actually incorporated fasting into their lives know about. Fasting, practiced scripturally, can have tremendous benefits both spiritually and physically. Putting it simply, here is the secret: Fasting, in general, aids us in keeping us humble enough to have a closer, more intimate relationship with God than during the times we are not fasting. Also, it is of utmost importance that fasting is combined with prayer, otherwise it would be no different than those who practice it for physical reasons only, such as to lose weight. So, fasting is not to try and force the hand of God to do anything, but is to help us get into that humble, spiritual frame of heart and mind where we can begin to experience the closest possible intimate fellowship with Him. To give us a reminder of the scriptural basis for fasting, I suggest reading the following references prayerfully in order to sense the impact and benefit fasting has had on God's people over centuries (emphases are mine):

"Then all the children of Israel, that is, all the people, went up and came to the house of God and wept. They sat there before the LORD and FASTED that day until evening; and they offered burnt offerings and peace offerings before the LORD" (Judges 20:26).

"So they gathered together at Mizpah, drew water, and poured it out before the Lord. And they FASTED that day, and said there, 'We have sinned against the Lord' " (1 Samuel 7:6).

"David therefore pleaded with God for the child, and David FASTED and went in and lay all night on the ground" (2 Samuel 12:16).

"All the valiant men arose and took the body of Saul and the bodies of his sons; and they brought them to Jabesh, and buried their bones under the tamarisk tree at Jabesh, and FASTED seven days" (1 Chronicles 10:12).

"Then I proclaimed a FAST there at the river of Ahava, that we might humble ourselves before our God, to seek from Him the right way for us and our little ones and all our possessions" (Ezra 8:21).

"So it was, when I heard these words, that I sat down and wept, and mourned for many days; I was FASTING and praying before the God of heaven" (Nehemiah 1:4).

"Go, gather all the Jews who are present in Shushan, and FAST for me; neither eat nor drink for three days, night or day. My maids and I will fast likewise. And so I will go to the king, which is against the law; and if I perish, I perish!" (Esther 4:16).

"I humbled myself with FASTING" (Psalm 35:13).

"Is this not the FAST that I have chosen: to loose the bonds of wickedness, to undo the heavy burdens, to let the oppressed go free, and that you break every yoke?" (Isaiah 58:6).

"Now it came to pass in the fifth year of Jehoiakim the son of Josiah, king of Judah, in the ninth month, that they proclaimed a FAST before the LORD to all the people in Jerusalem, and to all the people who came from the cities of Judah to Jerusalem" (Jeremiah 36:9).

"Then I set my face toward the Lord God to make request by prayer and supplications, with FASTING, sackcloth, and ashes" (Daniel 9:3).

"Now, therefore, says the LORD, Turn to Me with all your heart, with FASTING, with weeping, and with mourning" (Joel 2:12).

"So the people of Nineveh believed God, proclaimed a FAST, and put on sackcloth, from the greatest to the least of them" (Jonah 3:5).

"Say to all the people of the land, and to the priests: 'When you FASTED and mourned in the fifth and seventh months during those seventy years, did you really fast for Me—for Me?' " (Zechariah 7:5).

"And when He had FASTED forty days and forty nights, afterward He was hungry" (Matthew 4:2).

"Moreover, when you fast, do not be like the hypocrites, with a sad countenance. For they disfigure their faces that they may appear to men to be fasting. Assuredly, I say to you, they have their reward. But you, when you FAST, anoint your head and wash your face, so that you do not appear to men to be FASTING, but to your Father who is in the secret place; and your Father who sees in secret will reward you openly" (Matthew 6:16-18).

"However, this kind does not go out except by prayer and FASTING" (Matthew 17:21).

"And this woman was a widow of about eighty-four years, who did not depart from the temple, but served God with FASTINGS and prayers night and day" (Luke 2:37).

"As they ministered to the Lord and FASTED, the Holy Spirit said, 'Now separate to Me Barnabas and Saul for the work to which I have called them' " (Acts 13:2).

"So when they had appointed elders in every church, and prayed with FASTING, they commended them to the Lord in whom they had believed" (Acts 14:23).

"Do not deprive one another except with consent for a time, that you may give yourselves to FASTING and prayer; and come together again so that Satan does not tempt you because of your lack of self-control" (1 Corinthians 7:5).

"**In perils among false brethren; in weariness and toil, in sleeplessness often, in hunger and thirst, in FASTINGS often...**" (2 Corinthians 11:26,27).

After reading these scriptures we should be convinced of the need to incorporate fasting as part of our Christian experience and ministry to the Lord. The emphasis is to be on getting ourselves more spiritually sensitive to hear His voice and experience His fellowship more intimately. The Apostle John wrote, "**...and truly our fellowship *is* with the Father and with His Son Jesus Christ**" (1 John 1:3). If we are experiencing the closest spiritual relationship with our Lord that is possible during our daily lives, it follows that we will be more sensitive to knowing His will and direction. This is something that all Christians should desire, and often the question has been expressed: How can I be sure of God's will for my life? Or: How can I hear His voice of leading and guidance each day that I live? Fasting is a way that can provide answers to these questions. Pastor Jentezen Franklin speaks from experience when he writes:

"I am convinced that we will never walk in the perfect will of God until we seek Him through fasting. When you present your body in this manner, you open yourself up to hear from God. You will prove or discover His good and perfect will for your life. Paul was fasting when God called him and shared the assignment for his life (Acts 9:7-9). Peter was fasting on the rooftop when God gave him a new revelation and called him to take the gospel to the Gentiles (Acts 10). Fasting prepares the way for God to give you fresh revelation, fresh vision, and clear purpose.

In the Book of Joel, the Lord said, "And it shall come to pass afterward that I will pour out My Spirit on all flesh; your sons and your daughters shall prophesy, your old men shall dream dreams, your young men shall see visions" (Joel 2:28). God was going to pour out revival—*afterward*. He was revealing His will for His people—*afterward*. After what? After a fast. Israel was in sin, and God was calling His people to fast in repentance as a people: "Blow the trumpet in Zion, consecrate a fast" (v. 15). His promise to them was to pour out revival and blessings on the land.

I don't know about you, but I'm ready for those "afterward" seasons when God pours out revival...What are we waiting for when we read scriptures like 2 Chronicles 7:14? Can you imagine if believers in America really took hold of this, if they humbled themselves (fasted) and prayed? God would heal our nation and send revival" (Jentezen Franklin. *Fasting: Opening the Door to a Deeper, More Intimate, More Powerful Relationship With God.* Charisma House, Florida, 47,48 2008).

This is God's way. Just as it was God's way in the days of Joel, so it is His way for Christian believers today. Why does the Bible tell us to **"Humble yourselves in the sight of the Lord, and He will lift you up"** (James 4:10)? Because we are not inclined naturally to being humble, so our human nature needs help to come before the Lord with true humility. Anyone who has not fasted before will quickly find out its humbling effect after fasting for several days.

As mentioned above under the chapter title, the Apostle Paul wrote that he was **"In fastings often"** (2 Corinthians 11:27). He obviously understood the value of seeking the Lord through periods of fasting **"often."** This surely must mean more than once a year! I believe there must have been tremendous challenges facing him as he travelled and had so many different peoples to deal with while seeking to disciple young Christians in the newly established churches. He clearly must have found by experience that fasting was a necessary means of seeking the Lord and receiving the Spirit's guidance and direction. One of his great concerns, along with other spiritual leaders, was the need for unity among the believers.

Fasting is not an easy thing to do. One will soon find out the power of the stomach when it is suddenly deprived of all the good food it has been used to enjoying. But if the specific requests or needs we are fasting for are things drawing us into serious intercession, we will go ahead with the discipline of fasting in order that God will be glorified through the answers when they come.

But some may still be thinking: Is it really worth it? Does depriving myself really help me have a closer relationship with God? The answer to these questions is a definite "Yes." Let's remind ourselves again of the words of Jesus on this matter.

"But you, when you FAST, anoint your head and wash your face, so that you do not appear to men to be FASTING, but to your Father who is in the secret place; and your Father who sees in secret will reward you openly" (Matthew 6:16-18).

There is a temptation that many who practice fasting will encounter. It is the carnal soulish desire to impress others with the fact that you may have fasted for a specific number of days. Jesus teaches us that as much as possible our seeking Him through fasting and prayer should be a private matter. Of course, some close family members and friends will probably need to know about what you are doing, but determine in your heart that this is a time of special intimacy and relationship between you and your Lord. Remember that Jesus said to fast **"...in the secret place; and your Father who sees in secret will reward you openly."**

A few words about the practical aspects of fasting are appropriate here. Basically, fasting will either be with water only or what is usually called a Daniel fast which is mainly fruits and vegetables. On beginning a fast there will sometimes be physical discomforts such as headaches and feelings of weakness. These symptoms usually disappear by about the fourth day for most people. One should remember that these symptoms are evidence the body is beginning the process of cleansing and detoxification of all the toxins and impurities which in today's America almost everyone has. Whichever the type of fast chosen, it is extremely important to drink plenty of water. A fast of ten days or more for the average person in reasonable health will reap beneficial spiritual insights and physical wellbeing.

The challenge for us today is this: Do we have the same passion and concern for unity among God's people as the Lord does? If we do, we will surely use all the means at our disposal to aid in bringing to pass the will of God. God will answer prayer. Prayer combined with fasting is definitely one of the most powerful ways to gain lasting victories for the kingdom of God. Has the Spirit been speaking to your heart as He has to mine on this subject? Let us follow His leading and experience the victories that are ahead. Remember that Jesus said something that certainly does not sound as if it is optional for Christians:

"But the days will come when the bridegroom will be taken away from them, and then they will fast" (Matthew 9:15).

Chapter 21
We Can Be the Church God Wants Us to Be

"Husbands, love your wives, just as Christ also loved the church and gave Himself for her, that He might sanctify and cleanse her with the washing of the water by the word, that He might present her to Himself a glorious church, not having spot or wrinkle or any such thing, but that she should be holy and without blemish" (Ephesians 5:25-27).

"And He put all *things* under His feet, and gave Him *to be* head over all things to the church, which is His body, the fullness of Him who fills all in all" (Ephesians 1:22,23).

The Apostle Paul uses the most holy and sacred of human relationships, the marriage between a man and a woman, to express by illustration the relationship between Jesus and His Bride, the Church. It takes us back to the beginning when God made Eve from Adam's own body and decreed, **"Therefore a man shall leave his father and mother and be joined to his wife, and they shall become one flesh"** (Genesis 2:24). This is the foundation of God's plan for marriage to be the joining of one man and one woman for life.

Jesus loves the Church and died for it to come into existence. On the Day of Pentecost it did come into existence, and began with great and effective witness through the power of the Holy Spirit. But it is obvious that during many periods of history the Church has not become what it is supposed to be. In fact, if we know church history we could negatively say: The Church has often been a disaster! Was Jesus' sacrifice of no avail? When we see the lack of relationship among professed believers because of all the conspicuous ways and means by which we have visibly separated and isolated ourselves from one another, we could ask: How could Jesus find anything about the Church in general that would be exciting enough to love? We could also ask: How much patience does the Lord need to continue to expect His Church to become all that He has planned for her to be? Of course, we would have to say that such patience could only stem from the unfathomable grace and mercy of God.

Having said this, some self-examination would be in order. I have suddenly become aware of wondering how the Lord looks at my own participation as a member of His Church. How much patience does the Lord have to exercise and still consider me His close friend? Is my life bearing any fruit for Him and the kingdom of God in any way at all? Are there those who have looked at my life and went away encouraged by continuing the fight of faith, or conversely, have not been inspired by my example?

I believe we should all be introspective and seek the Lord earnestly until we are ready to let the Holy Spirit do His purging work in the depths of our spirit/soul beings. We are told to **"Examine yourselves, *as to* whether you are in the faith. Test yourselves"** (2 Corinthians 13:5). I have always tried to include a prayer for myself like this: Lord, tread on my toes as necessary, and show me where correction is needed. And another powerful prayer of mine has been: Lord, show me myself as *You* see me. Revelation that may come to us resulting from such transparency and sincere interaction with the Lord through prayer may turn out to be quite shocking. A scripture verse I do not remember hearing expounded on and applied to believers is Psalm 143:8b:

"Cause me to know the way in which I should walk, for I lift up my soul to You."

This verse would cause me to ask myself: Have I surrendered my *soul* to the Lord at the personal level? A broader question would include the Church: Has the body of Christ individually and corporately lifted up their *souls* to the Lord? What do these words **"lift up my soul"** mean?

The *soul* is described by many theologians as one of three interrelated areas of our inner spiritual beings; intellect (knowing, self-consciousness), will (decision), and emotion. This inner area within all of us can easily cause problems with keeping our relationship open and transparent with the Lord as it should be. At face value the Bible agrees that we are tripartite in nature. The Apostle Paul writes:

"Now may the God of peace Himself sanctify you completely; and may your whole spirit, soul, and body be preserved blameless at the coming of our Lord Jesus Christ" (1 Thessalonians 5:23).

The problem plaguing humans is that in our natural humanity we all tend to believe we know best on how to make decisions and deal with life's different situations. This would usually be through the reasoning of our intellects. However, as far as the universal Church is concerned, all the divisions that still exist in the body of Christ today remain as a testimony to our lack of success in producing and keeping observable spiritual unity with one another.

So, there must be a better way, and I believe this would be to individually surrender our entire being, spirit, soul and body to the Lord, and to seek His direction. In other words, let God lead us rather than attempting to lead ourselves. Over and over again in the Scriptures we see that Jesus submitted to the Father for direction in His ministry. For us, this always comes down to an individual commitment just as Jesus submitted His earthly life and ministry to the Father's leading and will. He said, **"The word that I speak to**

you I do not speak on My own *authority;* **but the Father who dwells in Me does the works"** (John 14:10).

For those with a heart for real spiritual unity there must be a willingness to surrender our intellects and our wills to Him. Regarding God's gift to us of our intellects, good education should be part of life and is necessary for obvious reasons. There is much to be commended in the desire to improve oneself through many different and beneficial intellectual pursuits. But the Bible brings us right back to the most important consideration of our desire for successful living when it says, **"The fear of the Lord** *is* **the beginning of wisdom, and the knowledge of the Holy One** *is* **understanding"** (Proverbs 9:10).

The truth is, just as in prayer for revival, a local church assembly can only become what the Lord wants it to become by starting with the spiritually open and yielded individuals within that fellowship. It will not just happen without individual believers taking hold of God with persistent and passionate prayer. As emphasized in the previous chapter, prayer with fasting is called for in obedience to the expectation of Jesus. Each one of us must look beyond ourselves. We must earnestly put into practice prayer for one another, and then we will begin to see all the members working together as a team for God's plan and purpose to be accomplished.

The question must be asked: Is there enough desire within church members to see the goal of Jesus for our oneness to become a reality? When it is a matter that concerns our desires we should be careful to note the words of Jesus. He said, **"If you abide in Me, and My words abide in you, you will ask what you desire, and it shall be done for you"** (John 15:7). **"...ask what you desire."** So, according to the promise of Jesus we have this amazing privilege of receiving what we ask for in prayer. However, before we rush ahead with our requests we should understand that the things we desire should always be within the boundary of God's will. This is why we must be sure to apply the *condition* of promises like this before we go overboard on asking things from God which may not be within the boundary of His will.

The conditions Jesus mentioned are: *abiding in Him,* and *His words abiding in us.* This is the secret contained in these words—if we abide or remain in Him as a continuing life style, *His desires will become our desires.* We must come to the place where we absolutely believe that His desires are better than our own. And if we believe this, we will submit to Him, which, of course, is obviously always the best and wisest thing to do.

Jesus has given us the conditions needed to be fulfilled in order to have such an intimate relationship with Him. When this becomes a living, experiential reality *His desires* will be infused into our inner spiritual beings. First, how do we *abide in Him?* There is an interesting account about a monk known as Brother Lawrence who was a resident in a monastery in Paris, France, in the 1600s. He wrote a short book titled, *The Practice of the Presence of God.* In his book he describes the struggles He had to keep an intimate relationship with the Lord on a daily basis. Among his duties in the monastery was washing all the pots and pans after each meal. This was a noisy, time-consuming job, and he wondered if he could ever overcome the distraction it caused that made it so difficult for him to continually be aware of God's presence. But as time went on, he was able to keep awareness of the Lord's presence even in noisy situations. In fact, he became known for the atmosphere of peace and the presence of the Lord that seemed to surround him.

To experience this myself I have had to realize that Brother Lawrence used the word "Practice" in the title of his book. In other words, it calls for concerted, purposeful discipline of my thought life. It has been something that I have been working on in my own life for many years. I am far from attaining anything even approaching the level of awareness of God's presence in my life that I would like, but with the Holy Spirit's help I have seen some success in this direction. Of course, we all know that Jesus said, **"I am with you always, even to the end of the age"** (Matthew 28:20). So, for example, I have now found it possible to be having a conversation with someone, and while I am speaking I can have the awareness of God's presence and trust the Holy Spirit for the very words I am speaking.

The Apostle Paul wrote about the presence of the Lord within us with these words: **"...that He would grant you, according to the riches of His glory, to be strengthened with might through His Spirit in the inner man, that Christ may dwell in your hearts through faith"** (Ephesians 3:16,17).

And again,

"Or do you not know that your body is the temple of the Holy Spirit who is in you, whom you have from God, and you are not your own? For you were bought at a price; therefore glorify God in your body and in your spirit, which are God's" (1 Corinthians 6:19,20).

So, we are told that **"Christ may dwell in our hearts through faith,"** and **"...your body is the temple of the Holy Spirit."** These are scriptures that we may be familiar with, but how many of us have entered into the reality of these scriptures by personal experience? How many of us have really grasped the wonder of these truths? I believe Jesus was always conscious of the Father's presence with Him, and this is why He could answer with the wisdom of God any who questioned Him. And question Him they did, with the intention of finding fault with Him and criticizing Him.

Being conscious of relying on the Lord's presence as we go through our daily lives will help us to be ready for all the various challenging situations we are sure to face. It will make so much difference and enable us to be able to present a truly Christ-like testimony to those with whom we interact. I believe that this concentration on individual growth and progress in our spiritual lives individually should help foster a spirit of unity among true believers corporately who are still connected to different streams of denominational beliefs.

This, then, is the challenge, to first look at our own lives individually in order to let the Lord deal with areas that need adjustment, and then to be willing for Him to mold us and fit us into the body of Christ according to His plan. It all depends on our willingness to be submissive and obedient to Him. Thank God that He has provided the remedy for us to have such a close relationship with our Creator after Adam and Eve had broken that relationship. It is all possible because Jesus Christ submitted Himself to the Father in obedience. The Book of Hebrews says of Jesus:

"...who, in the days of His flesh, when He had offered up prayers and supplications, with vehement cries and tears to Him who was able to save Him from death, and was heard because of His godly fear, though He was a Son, yet He learned obedience by the things which He suffered. And having been perfected, He became the author of eternal salvation to all who obey Him" Hebrews 5:7-9).

What a powerful insight this scripture is to the dramatic experience of the sufferings Jesus experienced while on this earth—even **"His godly fear."** This shows that although Jesus had limited Himself to a natural body for His earthly ministry, He still gave God the Father preeminence in His relationship with Him. Jesus suffered beyond our understanding, especially just before the crucifixion in the Garden of Gethsemane. But as the scripture says, He **"learned obedience."** This is the challenge for all of us, to *learn obedience.* Yes, we will suffer at times in our desire to follow the Lord without compromise, but there will also be times of great blessing and joy that will make it all more than worthwhile.

At the beginning of this chapter I quoted the scripture from Paul's Epistle to the Ephesians, and part of it reads: **"Husbands, love your wives, just as Christ also loved the church and gave Himself for her"** (Ephesians 5:25). Love is the key. It was the key for Jesus, and it will be the key for us. True, biblical, Spirit-inspired love will create harmony and gracious acceptance of one another in the body of Christ. How do we get to make this a reality? Again, it can only be by abiding in Christ and being obedient to His Word.

Question: would we be willing give our lives for the Church as Jesus did? Are we attempting to maintain independent control of our lives for personal and selfish reasons? Are we holding ourselves back from a too-close commitment to the Church? Maybe there are fears many of us need to overcome. Remember, Jesus gave His life for His Church. What an incredible privilege is ours to be a part of this divine fellowship with a glorious hope for the future. Next we will consider the amazing plan God has for all His children to experience personally.

Chapter 22
Be Filled With the Spirit

"Walk in the Spirit, and you shall not fulfill the lust of the flesh"
(Galatians 5:16).
"And do not be drunk with wine, in which is dissipation; but be filled with the Spirit"
(Ephesians 5:18).
"And they were all filled with the Holy Spirit"
(Acts 2:4).
"And when they had prayed, the place where they were assembled together was shaken; and they were all filled with the Holy Spirit, and they spoke word of God with boldness" (Acts 4:31).

I believe the ultimate solution for unity in the body of Christ is for every individual member to be experientially filled with the Holy Spirit. What would make more sense than this? Each member should be experiencing those rivers of living water streaming from within the inner spirit/soul being, to minister life to those around them. Jesus said, **"He who believes in Me, as the Scripture has said, out of his heart [KJV belly] will flow rivers of living water"** (John 7:38).

Many professed Christians may respond: I was *filled* with the Holy Spirit when I was saved. To this I would ask: What is the evidence in your life today for this to have been true? Of course, all Christians should understand that no one can begin their spiritual journey of salvation without the presence and involvement of the Holy Spirit. Why then, does the Apostle Paul exhort those who are *already Christians* to **"...be filled with the Spirit?"**

The reason for Paul's exhortation is because there is a difference and distinction between having the abiding presence of the Holy Spirit from the time of being born again, to having the enduement of supernatural power that Jesus also talked about in Luke 24:49:

"Behold, I send the Promise of My Father upon you; but tarry in the city of Jerusalem until you are endued with power from on high."

The word for **"power"** is the Greek word *dunamis* which relates to signs, wonders, and miracles such as healing and power over the works of darkness. This power is provided to us from the Lord to produce the ministry and works of God that He desires to accomplish through us. It is wonderful to know the inward joy and peace of sins forgiven and becoming new creations in Christ spiritually, but where is the evidence today of the kind of power we see in the experience of those early disciples?

Let us not reduce or compromise the plain, face-value meaning of a scripture like John 14:12 into something less than what it means and what Jesus intended for us to understand. He said:

"Most assuredly, I say to you, he who believes in Me, the works that I do he will do also; and greater *works* than these he will do, because I go to My Father."

What were these *works* of ministry Jesus did? He preached with power, and as mentioned above He healed the sick, cast out demons, raised the dead, and went around doing good. As Acts 10:38 confirms: **"...how God anointed Jesus of Nazareth with the Holy Spirit and with power, who went about doing good and healing all who were oppressed by the devil, for God was with Him."** Has God's plan for ministry changed since these early days? We obviously worship and serve the same God and the same Holy Spirit. Yet, much of Christian ministry today seems insipid and greatly lacking when compared to the ministry of those early believers in the Book of Acts.

Ministers and pastors preach clever sermons with no demonstration of the power of the Spirit to actually do the *works* that Jesus talked about. Why? There must be a missing ingredient. It would simply indicate that they are not filled with the power of the Spirit. This has to be the answer because Jesus said in Acts 1:8, **"But you shall receive power** [*dunamis*] **when the Holy Spirit has come upon you."** This is exactly what we see demonstrated when, after receiving this power of the mighty Holy Spirit, Peter, through faith and the leading of God, did the works of Jesus by healing the lame man at the entrance of the temple in Jerusalem. The result was that about 3000 very Jewish people believed Jesus was their Messiah and were saved and baptized. Now, to bring some balance to the above, there are certainly many times when pastors and teachers engaged in regular ministry are exercising their gifts with the aid of the Holy Spirit without any of the more dramatic manifestations of power.

However, I contend, based on a biblical foundation, that this is what we need today in our twenty-first century. We need Christians who are not satisfied just to be saved and in a living, active relationship with their Lord, as wonderful and important as this is. We need believers who are experientially filled with the power Jesus talked about that only the Holy Spirit can supply. We need Christians who actively demonstrate the power of the works of God in the daily marketplace outside the walls of church buildings as well as inside. In fact, I believe such demonstration of God's power should be more prevalent outside than inside! Only the Holy Spirit can give such boldness to those who have sought God and made themselves available for His service and ministry.

On the subject of *boldness,* consider these scriptures:

Now when they saw the boldness of Peter and John..." (Acts 4:13).

"...grant to Your servants that with all boldness they may speak Your word..." (Acts 4:29). Also, Acts 4:31 as above.

Why were these early disciples able to overcome natural fear and nervousness about obeying the Lord's command to be His witnesses? Simply stated, it was because they were all filled experientially with the Holy Spirit.

Question: How can we know we are filled with the Holy Spirit? Think of the 120 believers waiting in prayer for 10 days before the Day of Pentecost. Did they have any idea of what was going to happen? No! All they knew was that Jesus had promised them they would be baptized (immersed) with the Holy Spirit. But what would they have thought this to mean? However, after seeing manifestations of Jesus during the 40 days since the resurrection they knew the right course of action was simply to obey Him. Jesus told them they were going to receive something special from **"...the Father."** What an awesome thought, that they were going to have a connection with Almighty God, the Father, the Creator of all things in Heaven and Earth. The record says:

"And being assembled together with *them,* He commanded them not to depart from Jerusalem, but to wait for the Promise of the Father, 'Which,' *He said,* 'you have heard from Me; for John truly baptized with water, but you shall be baptized [Greek—immersed] **with the Holy Spirit not many days from now' "** (Acts 1:5).

But what happened to these 120 on the Day of Pentecost was something they could never have imagined. Significantly, this awesome event of the birth of the Christian Church occurred on a Sunday, the first day of the week, reminding us of the resurrection of Jesus. Referring to the Holy Spirit, Jesus had said to them, **"He dwells with you and will be in you"**

(John 14:17). The fulfillment of Jesus' promise of the Holy Spirit's power coming upon these 120 waiting believers was a very tangible, sensory, physical experience that was supernatural.

I can imagine these disciples and those waiting with them being absolutely awestruck when the sound of a violent wind suddenly descended upon them in that upper room. Then the supernatural appearance of what looked like tongues of fire hovered above each of them. This was truly an apparently one-time historical event to mark the birth of the Church. Each of the 120 experienced what I would call a surge of the Holy Spirit's power beginning to fill their spirit/soul beings with His powerful presence.

Based on my own personal experience as a young man I would imagine they literally felt a physical witness of wellbeing along with the Holy Spirit's spiritual enduement of power. When this happened to me I was overwhelmed with the realization of the awesome presence of God through the Holy Spirit, and I literally felt a glowing warmth beginning from somewhere deep in my abdomen that proceeded to flood my whole physical being. My eyes were streaming with tears, and I felt a depth of joy and peace I had never experienced before. Remember, at this time I had been a born again believer in Jesus Christ for eight years. Why did eight years of my Christian life pass before I had the experience of being filled with the Spirit? A pertinent factor was obviously because I had never been taught this truth from God's Word. My church experience for those eight years did not mention the biblical truth that Christians today can experience being filled with the Holy Spirit in a similar way to those early disciples. However, when a Christian mentioned this to me I began to search the Scriptures for myself until I was convinced this would be something the Lord would want me to experience, and that it would be for the glory of God.

Before I experienced this blessing of the Holy Spirit in my life I was an extremely shy individual. I could not speak any words publicly unless I was reading them. And even then my heart would be racing with nervousness. However, after this experience I was not afraid to speak publicly but actually wanted to speak, and especially to teach the Word of God. It was during this period of my life as a young man in my early twenties that I sensed a call to ministry from the Lord. Actually, according to Scripture, all Christians have a call to ministry and God will lead each one into the special place planned for them in the body of Christ.

From my own experience I can testify that God has helped me to be able to accept true brothers and sisters in Christ regardless of their different expressions of worship and teachings that arise from various church backgrounds. This is not to say I would agree with others on every doctrinal detail because my own understanding of Scripture on certain matters would probably differ. The main thing to look for is genuine, intimate relationship with the Triune God of the Bible, and evidence of passion for the fulfilling of the call of the Gospel in obedience to the commands of Jesus. If God's people are *filled with the Spirit* I believe we can see amazing renewal and revival as unity of purpose becomes a reality. "Keeping the main thing the main thing" is an exhortation that many preachers have used in their sermons. It is good advice. God wants the **"whoever believes"** (John 3:16) to be as many souls as possible. I have to challenge myself with this question: Is my life bearing fruit for Him to this end? How about you?

George Whitefield (1714-1770), was greatly used of God in the revival days of the Great Awakening, and loved to tell of an imaginary conversation with Abraham to express his passion for the mission of the Church as follows:

"George Whitefield spoke for Evangelicals of every generation when, preaching from the courthouse balcony in Philadelphia, he raised his eyes to the heavens and cried out: 'Father Abraham, whom have you in heaven? Any Episcopalians? No! Any Presbyterians? No! Any Independents or Methodists? No, no, no! Whom have you there? We don't know those names here. All who are here are Christians....Oh, is this the case? Then God help us to forget party names and to become Christians in deed and truth' " (Bruce Shelley, *Church History in Plain Language*, Word Publishing, Dallas, Texas. 1995 448,449).

Good counsel! Can we follow it? God bless you all.
Rod Butterworth

OTHER BOOKS BY Dr. Rod Butterworth

Available on Amazonbooks.com

Enter in search box: Rod Butterworth books

Did God Really Say That?: Creation and Biblical Authority.
Found Wanting: America Needs Revival Now.
Walking With God.
There is Hope for America: If My People.
Can I Be Pure: Holy Living in a Corrupt World.

You can also here Dr. Butterworth's teachings on YouTube.

Enter: Rod Butterworth in YouTube search box.
Ministry website: creationexperiencemuseum.com